MODERN WORLD LEADERS

# Vladimir Putin

# MODERN WORLD LEADERS

Tony Blair
George W. Bush
Hugo Chávez
Pope Benedict XVI
Pope John Paul II
The Saudi Royal Family
Vladimir Putin

## MODERN WORLD LEADERS

# Vladimir Putin

Charles J. Shields
With additional text by Brenda Lange

CHELSEA HOUSE
PUBLISHERS
An imprint of Infobase Publishing

**Vladimir Putin**

Chelsea House
An imprint of Infobase Publishing
132 West 31st Street
New York, NY 10001

**Library of Congress Cataloging-in-Publication Data**

Shields, Charles J., 1951–
  Vladimir Putin / Charles J. Shields.
     p. cm. — (Modern world leaders)
  Includes bibliographical references and index.
  ISBN 0-7910-9215-1 (hardcover)
  1. Putin, Vladimir Vladimirovich, 1952—Juvenile literature. 2. Presidents—Russia (Federation)—Biography—Juvenile literature. 3. Russia (Federation)—Politics and government—1991—Juvenile literature. I. Title. II. Series.
  DK510.766.P87S54 2006
  947.086092—dc22            2006013657

Text design by Erik Lindstrom
Cover design by Takeshi Takahashi

Printed in the United States of America

Bang FOF 10 9 8 7 6 5 4 3 2 1

This book is printed on acid-free paper.

All links and Web addresses were checked and verified to be correct at the time of publication. Because of the dynamic nature of the Web, some addresses and links may have changed since publication and may no longer be valid.

# TABLE OF CONTENTS

## Arthur M. Schlesinger, Jr.
# On Leadership

Leadership, it may be said, is really what makes the world go round. Love no doubt smoothes the passage; but love is a private transaction between consenting adults. Leadership is a public transaction with history. The idea of leadership affirms the capacity of individuals to move, inspire, and mobilize masses of people so that they act together in pursuit of an end. Sometimes leadership serves good purposes, sometimes bad; but whether the end is benign or evil, great leaders are those men and women who leave their personal stamp on history.

Now, the very concept of leadership implies the proposition that individuals can make a difference. This proposition has never been universally accepted. From classical times to the present day, eminent thinkers have regarded individuals as no more than the agents and pawns of larger forces, whether the gods and goddesses of the ancient world or, in the modern era, race, class, nation, the dialectic, the will of the people, the spirit of the times, history itself. Against such forces, the individual dwindles into insignificance.

So contends the thesis of historical determinism. Tolstoy's great novel *War and Peace* offers a famous statement of the case. Why, Tolstoy asked, did millions of men in the Napoleonic Wars, denying their human feelings and their common sense, move back and forth across Europe slaughtering their fellows? "The war," Tolstoy answered, "was bound to happen simply because it was bound to happen." All prior history determined it. As for leaders, they, Tolstoy said, "are but the labels that serve to give a name to an end and, like labels, they have the least possible connection with the event." The greater the leader, "the more conspicuous the inevitability and the predestination of every act he commits." The leader, said Tolstoy, is "the slave of history."

Determinism takes many forms. Marxism is the determinism of class. Nazism the determinism of race. But the idea of men and women as the slaves of history runs athwart the deepest human instincts. Rigid determinism abolishes the idea of human freedom—the assumption of free choice that underlies every move we make, every word we speak, every thought we think. It abolishes the idea of human responsibility, since it is manifestly unfair to reward or punish people for actions that are by definition beyond their control. No one can live consistently by any deterministic creed. The Marxist states prove this themselves by their extreme susceptibility to the cult of leadership.

More than that, history refutes the idea that individuals make no difference. In December 1931, a British politician crossing Fifth Avenue in New York City between 76th and 77th streets around 10:30 P.M. looked in the wrong direction and was knocked down by an automobile—a moment, he later recalled, of a man aghast, a world aglare: "I do not understand why I was not broken like an eggshell or squashed like a gooseberry." Fourteen months later an American politician, sitting in an open car in Miami, Florida, was fired on by an assassin; the man beside him was hit. Those who believe that individuals make no difference to history might well ponder whether the next two decades would have been the same had Mario Constasino's car killed Winston Churchill in 1931 and Giuseppe Zangara's bullet killed Franklin Roosevelt in 1933. Suppose, in addition, that Lenin had died of typhus in Siberia in 1895 and that Hitler had been killed on the western front in 1916. What would the twentieth century have looked like now?

For better or for worse, individuals do make a difference. "The notion that a people can run itself and its affairs anonymously," wrote the philosopher William James, "is now well known to be the silliest of absurdities. Mankind does nothing save through initiatives on the part of inventors, great or small, and imitation by the rest of us—these are the sole factors in human progress. Individuals of genius show the way, and set the patterns, which common people then adopt and follow."

Leadership, James suggests, means leadership in thought as well as in action. In the long run, leaders in thought may well make the greater difference to the world. "The ideas of economists and political philosophers, both when they are right and when they are wrong," wrote John Maynard Keynes, "are more powerful than is commonly understood. Indeed the world is ruled by little else. Practical men, who believe themselves to be quite exempt from any intellectual influences, are usually the slaves of some defunct economist. . . . The power of vested interests is vastly exaggerated compared with the gradual encroachment of ideas."

But, as Woodrow Wilson once said, "Those only are leaders of men, in the general eye, who lead in action. . . . It is at their hands that new thought gets its translation into the crude language of deeds." Leaders in thought often invent in solitude and obscurity, leaving to later generations the tasks of imitation. Leaders in action—the leaders portrayed in this series—have to be effective in their own time.

And they cannot be effective by themselves. They must act in response to the rhythms of their age. Their genius must be adapted, in a phrase from William James, "to the receptivities of the moment." Leaders are useless without followers. "There goes the mob," said the French politician, hearing a clamor in the streets. "I am their leader. I must follow them." Great leaders turn the inchoate emotions of the mob to purposes of their own. They seize on the opportunities of their time, the hopes, fears, frustrations, crises, potentialities. They succeed when events have prepared the way for them, when the community is awaiting to be aroused, when they can provide the clarifying and organizing ideas. Leadership completes the circuit between the individual and the mass and thereby alters history.

It may alter history for better or for worse. Leaders have been responsible for the most extravagant follies and most monstrous crimes that have beset suffering humanity. They have also been vital in such gains as humanity has made in individual freedom, religious and racial tolerance, social justice, and respect for human rights.

There is no sure way to tell in advance who is going to lead for good and who for evil. But a glance at the gallery of men and women in MODERN WORLD LEADERS suggests some useful tests.

One test is this: Do leaders lead by force or by persuasion? By command or by consent? Through most of history leadership was exercised by the divine right of authority. The duty of followers was to defer and to obey. "Theirs not to reason why/Theirs but to do and die." On occasion, as with the so-called enlightened despots of the eighteenth century in Europe, absolutist leadership was animated by humane purposes. More often, absolutism nourished the passion for domination, land, gold, and conquest and resulted in tyranny.

The great revolution of modern times has been the revolution of equality. "Perhaps no form of government," wrote the British historian James Bryce in his study of the United States, *The American Commonwealth*, "needs great leaders so much as democracy." The idea that all people should be equal in their legal condition has undermined the old structure of authority, hierarchy, and deference. The revolution of equality has had two contrary effects on the nature of leadership. For equality, as Alexis de Tocqueville pointed out in his great study *Democracy in America*, might mean equality in servitude as well as equality in freedom.

"I know of only two methods of establishing equality in the political world," Tocqueville wrote. "Rights must be given to every citizen, or none at all to anyone . . . save one, who is the master of all." There was no middle ground "between the sovereignty of all and the absolute power of one man." In his astonishing prediction of twentieth-century totalitarian dictatorship, Tocqueville explained how the revolution of equality could lead to the *Führerprinzip* and more terrible absolutism than the world had ever known.

But when rights are given to every citizen and the sovereignty of all is established, the problem of leadership takes a new form, becomes more exacting than ever before. It is easy to issue commands and enforce them by the rope and the stake, the concentration camp and the *gulag*. It is much harder to use argument and achievement to overcome opposition and win consent. The Founding Fathers of the United States understood the difficulty. They believed that history had given them the opportunity to decide, as Alexander Hamilton wrote in the first Federalist Paper, whether men are indeed capable of basing government on "reflection and choice, or whether they are forever destined to depend . . . on accident and force."

Government by reflection and choice called for a new style of leadership and a new quality of followership. It required leaders to be responsive to popular concerns, and it required followers to be active and informed participants in the process. Democracy does not eliminate emotion from politics; sometimes it fosters demagoguery; but it is confident that, as the greatest of democratic leaders put it, you cannot fool all of the people all of the time. It measures leadership by results and retires those who overreach or falter or fail.

It is true that in the long run despots are measured by results too. But they can postpone the day of judgment, sometimes indefinitely, and in the meantime they can do infinite harm. It is also true that democracy is no guarantee of virtue and intelligence in government, for the voice of the people is not necessarily the voice of God. But democracy, by assuring the right of opposition, offers built-in resistance to the evils inherent in absolutism. As the theologian Reinhold Niebuhr summed it up, "Man's capacity for justice makes democracy possible, but man's inclination to justice makes democracy necessary."

A second test for leadership is the end for which power is sought. When leaders have as their goal the supremacy of a master race or the promotion of totalitarian revolution or the acquisition and exploitation of colonies or the protection of greed and privilege or the preservation of personal power, it is likely that their leadership will do little to advance the cause of humanity. When their goal is the abolition of slavery, the liberation of women, the enlargement of opportunity for the poor and powerless, the extension of equal rights to racial minorities, the defense of the freedoms of expression and opposition, it is likely that their leadership will increase the sum of human liberty and welfare.

Leaders have done great harm to the world. They have also conferred great benefits. You will find both sorts in this series. Even "good" leaders must be regarded with a certain wariness. Leaders are not demigods; they put on their trousers one leg after another just like ordinary mortals. No leader is infallible, and every leader needs to be reminded of this at regular intervals. Irreverence irritates leaders but is their salvation. Unquestioning submission corrupts leaders and demeans followers. Making a cult of a leader is always a mistake. Fortunately hero worship generates its own antidote. "Every hero," said Emerson, "becomes a bore at last."

The single benefit the great leaders confer is to embolden the rest of us to live according to our own best selves, to be active, insistent, and resolute in affirming our own sense of things. For great leaders attest to the reality of human freedom against the supposed inevitabilities of history. And they attest to the wisdom and power that may lie within the most unlikely of us, which is why Abraham Lincoln remains the supreme example of great leadership. A great leader, said Emerson, exhibits new possibilities to all humanity. "We feed on genius. . . . Great men exist that there may be greater men."

Great leaders, in short, justify themselves by emancipating and empowering their followers. So humanity struggles to master its destiny, remembering with Alexis de Tocqueville: "It is true that around every man a fatal circle is traced beyond which he cannot pass; but within the wide verge of that circle he is powerful and free; as it is with man, so with communities." ●

# 1

# A Modern Leader

**FOR GENERATIONS, RUSSIAN PEOPLE HAVE HAD TO ADAPT TO VARIOUS FORMS** of government. In recent history, this has covered the spectrum from monarchy to Communism to the current democracy. Today, under the administration of the country's third democratically elected president, Vladimir Putin, the Russian people have more choices and a louder voice in how their country is run.

Under Communism, people were not allowed to practice the religion of their choice, were unable to speak freely without fear of retribution by the government, and were not even allowed to read or write whatever they wished. Since the fall of the Soviet Union, churches have gradually reopened, previously banned books are back on the shelves, and the country's ancient heritage is once again being honored throughout the country and around the world.

The change has not come easily and some of the country's growing pains have been violent, including uprisings in Chechnya, a region in the northern Caucasus Mountains, which has been trying to declare its independence from Russia since 1991. Chechnya plays a vital economic role for Russia because of several oil and gas pipelines located there. The Russian government also claims that the region, by its constitution, does not have the right to secede.

Terrorism has hit the country as well, killing thousands. A particularly brutal event took place in the small village of Beslan on September 1, 2004, when Chechen rebels took hundreds of schoolchildren and their parents and teachers hostage in a school. The outcome of the siege was tragic, with more than 300 killed, mostly children. Another noteworthy event was the storming of a theater in Moscow that left many dead. Intermittently, suicide bombings have claimed the lives of diplomats and civil servants as well as innocent civilians.

After the terrorist attacks on the United States on September 11, 2001, Putin was the first foreign leader to call President George W. Bush to offer his condolences and help. The old "hotline" from the days of the Cold War was still in operation, and Putin utilized this connection to reach Bush on Air Force One just hours after the towers fell.

Putin has remained committed to eradicating worldwide terrorism and has developed a close friendship with Bush, even though the two men don't agree on everything, including the Kyoto Treaty and Bush's review of U.S. assistance programs and policies to the Russians. The key to their friendship is found in the belief that terrorism is the worst possible threat to international security. Putin proved his friendship when he pledged "active intelligence cooperation" with the United States. To fulfill this promise, he provided secret information on the topography and caves in Afghanistan and other data that helped U.S. Special Forces find their way around the capital city of Kabul in search of Taliban fighters.

This unconditional support for the United States was a new experience for the Russian people. Putin asked for

During the Beslan school siege on September 1, 2004, police officers take cover behind their car. Four hundred people were taken hostage, and about 300 were killed, mostly children.

nothing in return, which was also a new role for Russia, and one that surprised the rest of the world.

Improvements in Russia under Putin include economic reforms that have resulted in the rise in quality of life for many. But his approach is still based on personal power, which causes some tension between him and the governments of other countries. According to Jessica Mathews, president of the Carnegie Endowment for International Peace, "He has attempted to base his rule on a mix—economic liberalism, pragmatic authoritarianism, and a pro-Western orientation." She explains that this mix may not be sufficient to deal with his country in its postindustrial era. In order for his approach to work, he will need to allow government to expand.

# 2

# A Wall Comes Down

IN A LARGE GRAY HOUSE AT NO. 4 ANGELIKASTRASSE, OR ANGEL STREET, IN Dresden, East Germany, a young major in the Soviet secret police watched one of the most powerful countries on earth—his own—fall apart in November 1989. The major's name was Vladimir V. Putin.

The 37-year-old Putin was a spy. His job was to look for professors, journalists, scientists, or technicians who would be traveling from Communist East Germany to the non-Communist West on business. He would try to recruit them to serve his goal, which was to steal technology or secrets from pro-Western governments.

He was a patriot. His parents had been decorated for heroism during the siege of Leningrad from September 1941 to January 1944 because they helped expel the Nazi invaders. An estimated one million citizens had died during the 900-day siege, including Putin's older brother, whom he never knew.

According to the *Washington Post*, when asked once why he would not read a book written by a Soviet defector (someone who had fled to the West), Putin replied, "I don't read books by people who have betrayed the Motherland."

Now, as Putin listened to the news filtering into his office, it was clear that the Union of Soviet Socialist Republics (USSR) was no longer a soviet, or council of revolutionary groups, or even a union at all. Countries that had been swallowed by the USSR were declaring independence.

Rumor had it that even in Romania, the days of iron-fisted Communist dictator Nicolae Ceausescu were numbered. In fact, in just a few weeks, pro-democracy demonstrators would haul Ceausescu and his wife before a hastily convened court on Christmas Day and accuse them of being enemies of the Romanian people. When the haughty pair refused to reply, their captors took them outside. They were shoved against a wall and executed by a firing squad.

That November, as Putin looked out the windows of his office overlooking the Elbe River, he must have wondered what the future held for him. Perhaps East Germany, where he was serving, would remain stable. It had been the cornerstone of the Eastern Communist bloc. For months now, East German leader Erich Honecker had been denying that anything was wrong and claiming that East Germany was still solidly under Soviet control.

He was too knowledgeable and too smart to really believe that, though. Events unfolding in East and West Berlin, the divided capital of Germany, were proving otherwise. He "must have noticed the system did not work anymore," a German specialist later told the *Washington Post*. "If he was not stupid he would have noticed the East Germans were the losers of economic history."

Thousands of pro-democracy East German demonstrators, tired of their economy running down, of industrial pollution poisoning the air and water, of a police state that crushed individual freedoms, had taken to the streets in 1989. Putin had felt their anger come dangerously close when a crowd attacked his office, the headquarters of the secret police in Dresden. With the mob jeering in the background, he had been forced to phone the East German Soviet military command for emergency assistance. *New York Times* reporter Celestine Bohlen reported that the voice on the other end replied, "We cannot do anything without orders from Moscow. And Moscow is silent." The words haunted Putin. The Soviet Union seemed to be disappearing. Even in Berlin, where the democratic West and the Communist East had faced off for more than 40 years, the Soviets seemed unable to hang on. At this rate, Russia, where the Communist revolution had begun in 1917, would stand alone, stripped of its allies.

Putin had built his career on fighting for the Communist side—or, more personally, the motherland, Russia—in the Cold War. Now all that was changing. A new tide in history was rising. He would have to find the direction of its current and go with it.

## THE COLD WAR

*Cold War* was a term coined shortly after the end of World War II to describe the intense rivalry between Communist and non-Communist nations. Pitted against the USSR and its Communist allies were the United States and its democratic allies. Because actual world war or "hot" war had been avoided year after year, the struggle came to be known as the Cold War instead.

Before the end of World War II, it seemed as if a spirit of friendship might develop between the United States and the Soviet Union, especially during the months that led up to Germany's surrender in May 1945. At the February 1945 Yalta Conference attended by President Franklin D. Roosevelt of the United States, Prime Minister Winston Churchill of Great Britain, and Premier Joseph Stalin of the Soviet Union, a

At the Yalta Conference in February 1945, the so-called Big Three—(seated, from left to right) British Prime Minister Winston Churchill, U.S. President Franklin Roosevelt, and Soviet Premier Joseph Stalin—made plans for the organization of Europe after World War II.

peace plan emerged that would be followed after the war. The Big Three, as the leaders were called, agreed to set up occupation zones (areas controlled by the Allies) to manage postwar Germany. They also developed the Declaration on Liberated Europe, in which they pledged to hold democratic elections in countries freed from the control of Germany and its allies. In addition, the first steps were taken for forming the United Nations—an institution that could prevent conflict by mediating international issues. Within just one year after the Yalta Conference, however, relations between the United States and the Soviet Union began to deteriorate.

When Stalin agreed to the Declaration on Liberated Europe, Soviet forces had already driven the German army out of most of Eastern Europe. The USSR occupied the Baltic states of Latvia, Estonia, and Lithuania; parts of Poland, Finland, and

Romania; and eastern Czechoslovakia. Soviet troops also occupied a third of Germany and all of Bulgaria, Hungary, Poland, and Romania. At the Potsdam Conference in July 1945, Western nations reluctantly agreed to go along with the Soviets' idea to transfer 40,000 square miles of German territory to Polish control. After that, with hundreds of thousands of troops in place across Eastern Europe, Stalin had no intention of throwing away his military and political advantage.

## THE SOVIETS CREATE A COMMUNIST EMPIRE

As soon as the war ended, in the name of security, Stalin moved swiftly. The Kremlin in Moscow—the seat of Soviet power—installed a pro-Communist government in Poland because the Nazis had used Poland as a route to invade the Soviet Union. Ignoring Western protests, Stalin severed almost all contact between the West and the occupied territories of Eastern Europe during 1945 and early in 1946. The Cold War, never officially declared, was under way.

With astonishing speed, countries became Soviet satellites, or nations controlled by the USSR. Albania had already turned Communist in 1944. Yugoslavia had also joined the Communist bloc after the Communist Party of Yugoslavia had helped drive out the Germans near the end of the war. In 1946, the Soviets organized Communist governments in Bulgaria and Romania. In 1947, Communist groups took control of Hungary and Poland. Communists seized full power in Czechoslovakia in early 1948. The Eastern European countries all seemed to be falling into the Soviet sphere of power.

In March 1946, British prime minister Winston Churchill delivered a speech in which he said that an "iron curtain" separated the Communist nations of Eastern Europe from the democratic nations of the West. The term "iron curtain" came to be a common way to describe the division of nations during the Cold War.

## In people's imaginations, the Iron Curtain became a vivid metaphor—one that fully explained the political barrier that existed between the East and West.

In a speech delivered at Westminster College in Fulton, Missouri, in March 1946, Churchill warned, "An iron curtain has descended across the Continent. Behind that line lie all the capitals of the ancient states of Central and Eastern Europe."

The United States responded with a "get tough" policy to try to "stop the spread of Communism"—a widely used phrased in the 1950s and 1960s. The Soviet Union counterattacked by accusing the West of trying to encircle it and overthrow its form of government.

In people's imaginations, the Iron Curtain became a vivid metaphor—one that fully explained the political barrier that existed between the East and West. No one expected that an actual, physical barrier would be constructed to separate the East from the West, but that was what happened in Berlin on August 13, 1961.

### THE BERLIN WALL

At the Yalta Conference, Roosevelt, Churchill, and Stalin had divided Germany into four zones, with the United States, Soviet Union, Great Britain, and France each occupying a zone. The four powers jointly administered the city of Berlin, which lay deep within the Soviet zone of Germany. Eventually, the three non-Communist powers combined their three West Berlin zones into one.

In 1948, as part of its drive to consolidate control over Eastern Europe, the Soviet Union tried to drive the Western allies out of Berlin. Soviet troops blocked all rail, water, and highway routes, isolating West Berlin from allied support. For over a year, under the Marshall Plan, the Western allies flew in food, medical supplies, fuel, and other goods to prevent the city from falling into Soviet hands. The Soviet Union finally lifted the Berlin blockade in May 1949, and the airlift ended in September. Although the immediate crisis was over, Berlin had become an international symbol of the East-West contest.

After 1948, life in West Berlin was better than in East Berlin, and the contrast was stark. From 1949 to 1961, 2.6 million East Berliners and East Germans fled the Communist regime by illegally entering West Germany. In June 1961, Soviet leader Nikita Khrushchev demanded of U.S. president John F. Kennedy that the Western powers pull their troops out of Berlin. He promised to do the same, but the two leaders failed to reach an agreement. Then, in July, the USSR ominously increased its military spending.

On Saturday afternoon, August 12, Berliners noticed an increase in troops and vehicles along the checkpoints dividing the city's eastern side from the western side. At 4:00 P.M., Walter Ulbricht, the East German leader, signed commands to close the border. That night, as the politically divided nation slept, Soviet-led soldiers began to tear up streets and install wire fences. By morning, Berlin had been cut in two.

Within a few months, the wire fences had become a concrete wall—26 miles long and built of massive concrete slabs from 12 to 15 feet high. The wall ran through the center of the city, through train stations, parks, and even cemeteries. The Soviets ringed the perimeter of East Berlin, too, as if it were a giant fortress, and the length of the wall reached 110 miles. To confirm the right of the Western powers to remain in West Berlin, the United States sent troops into the city by highway, protected by tanks. Still, the work on the wall continued. The Soviets dug 65 miles of anti-vehicle trenches, built 20 fortified bunkers, erected 302 watch towers, and strung 41 miles of wire mesh fencing.

The East Berlin checkpoints bristled with armed guards, guard dogs, barbed wire, gates, electric alarms, and even mines.

East Germans who dared to cross the wall risked death. Soviet soldiers had shoot-to-kill orders. Some refugees tried to leap over the top of the wall at first; others tried to tunnel under it. Over the years, 192 persons were shot dead at the wall, 200 were injured by gunfire, and 3,200 were arrested in the border area.

The first steps were taken toward dividing the city of Berlin in half to separate the Communist East from the democratic West. About 5,000 people successfully made it across, including one East German guard who suddenly leaped over his checkpoint gate and fled into West Berlin.

## THE USSR BEGINS TO WEAKEN

When Putin joined the Soviet secret police, or KGB, in 1975, he was part of a legacy of mistrust between the United States and the USSR. The Berlin Wall was the Cold War's monument. But, by the late 1980s, anyone in the Soviet Union—certainly someone as keen on politics as Putin—could see that deep cracks were starting to appear in the Communist bloc.

There was, for instance, the meeting in December 1988 of Soviet leader Mikhail Gorbachev, U.S. president Ronald Reagan, and his successor, George Bush Sr. In a surprise move, Gorbachev announced that the people of Eastern Europe had the right of self-determination. Privately, Gorbachev had decided that the Cold War must end, but his offer to loosen the reins on Soviet allies in the Eastern bloc still startled the international community. The West responded with a skeptical wait-and-see attitude.

The first test came in the summer of 1989. East Germans, hearing that the border with the West was weakening, rushed to take vacations in Hungary. In the capital city of Budapest, the West German embassy was suddenly besieged with East German "vacationers" demanding help to emigrate. East

German leader Erich Honecker condemned these people as outcasts of society. When refugees stubbornly crammed themselves into the embassy and refused to leave, Honecker, under pressure from the Kremlin, was forced to backpedal. The refugees were free to go to West Germany, he said, but they would first have to pass through East Germany by train. That way, at least, he could claim he was expelling them and canceling their citizenship.

Honecker seemed to be the only major figure who could not see that his control over East Germany was slipping. In power since 1971, he had been described as "invincible" as late as 1985. Despite this confidence in his power, another embarrassing challenge to his authority came on the heels of the mass emigration in the autumn of 1989.

As Honecker welcomed Gorbachev to East Berlin in October during an East German anniversary celebration, crowds of demonstrators rushed the parade route. At first, they shouted rehearsed slogans, but when they saw Gorbachev, according to news agency CNN, they spontaneously began to chant, "Gorby, save us! Gorby, save us!" Honecker realized it was critical to show that he was still in control. His chance came two days later.

### THE BERLIN WALL FALLS

A protest rally calling for the reunification of East and West Germany, and the creation of a new democratic government, was planned in Leipzig. Honecker put the East German army on high alert, and the city went into a state of emergency. When the number of marchers in the streets reached 70,000, the Soviet ambassador in Leipzig panicked. He phoned the commander of the Soviet forces in the region and warned him to use restraint or there could be a civil uprising. The warning came too late. Without orders, Leipzig officials pulled back all police and troops. The protest went off peacefully. In full view of the free world, the Soviet system was breaking down.

Early in the morning on November 11, 1989, hundreds of Berlin residents climbed atop the Berlin Wall to make a dramatic demand that the wall—long a symbol of political oppression and the tensions of the Cold War—be torn down.

Honecker, once the model of Soviet sternness, now seemed out of step with the times. On October 17, the East German Politburo (legislature) voted him out of power. In his place, they chose Egon Krenz, a moderate. Krenz immediately went on record to promise democratic reforms. When he traveled to Moscow on November 1, he was heartened to hear Gorbachev urge him to ease travel restrictions to the West. On November 9, 1989, an East German government official announced to journalists that travel restrictions would indeed be lifted. What he failed to add was that they would be lifted the following day. As it turned out, the desire for freedom could not wait.

The news of the eased restrictions flashed around the city. Thousands of East Germans rushed to the Berlin Wall to see if it was true, if the checkpoints were down, if West Berlin was open again for the first time since 1961. Border guards, who had no orders but to prevent anyone from escaping, saw the throngs of East Germans growing larger. To resist the sea of people surging against the wall would be futile. Suddenly, the gates at the checkpoints rose and joyful East Berliners began to pour through. Those who could not wait to go through the gates began to climb over the hated concrete barrier. As then President George Bush later described it, "Freedom was literally cascading over the wall." West Berliners arrived from the other direction and began to demolish the wall with picks and hammers in front of the 200-year-old Brandenburg Gate, long a symbol of German nationalism. Germany was reuniting in spirit, if not yet officially.

## THE END OF THE COLD WAR

In Dresden, at his post with the secret police, Putin must have known that the events of early November had turned him overnight into a relic of the past. He had been a Cold War fighter, but the old battle lines had collapsed. What point was there to lurk around undercover, to recruit spies to steal secrets from the West, when the East and West were flowing into each other?

The Berlin Wall had burst like a dam and democracy was running like a river into the countries that had been parched by Communism for a generation. Putin would have to trade in his uniform for a civilian suit and find his way to the new centers of power, where East and West would soon be overlapping. On the night the Berlin Wall collapsed, Putin was busy destroying secret documents, stuffing so many into the flames of a stove that it burst.

In December, on a ship off the coast of Malta, Gorbachev met with George Bush for a private summit and was quoted by CNN as saying, "We don't consider you an enemy anymore."

A year later, when Germany was reunited, Putin left Dresden. He had accepted a new post. He headed home to Russia, as if starting over, to the city of his birth—Leningrad.

# 3

# The Boy Who Wanted to Be a Spy

**IN THE FLICKERING DARKNESS OF A LENINGRAD MOVIE THEATER IN 1968,** ninth-grader Vladimir Putin—nicknamed "Putka" by his friends—found his calling in life. On the screen was a Russian-made film, *The Sword and the Shield*. It was the story of a heroic Soviet double agent in Nazi Germany. As he watched the story unfold, Putka could think of nothing grander or more admirable than being a spy. The job was all about courage, about risking one's life for love of country. He wondered how someone got to play such a role in real life. According to CNN.com, he recalled, "It seemed so unattainable, like flying to Mars." On the other hand, the traits he needed might just be in his blood.

## THE PUTIN FAMILY

His father, Vladimir Spirdonovich Putin, had volunteered for submarine duty against the Germans in World War II. Later, he was assigned to a demolitions battalion engaged in sabotage and was dropped behind the German lines in Estonia. When enemy sympathizers betrayed his unit, he escaped capture by submerging himself in a swamp and breathing through a hollow reed. Out of 28 men, only he and 4 others survived. Sent back into combat, he was ordered to capture a German soldier for interrogation. He crawled over the ground as close as he could get to the enemy position, but suddenly a German spotted him and tossed a grenade. Shrapnel from the explosion tore up his legs. Hours later, a comrade carried him across the frozen Neva River to the only available hospital.

Meanwhile, Putin's mother, Maria, was trapped in Leningrad, a city under siege by the German army. Married to her husband when they were both 17, she was poorly educated and unskilled. As the Germans tried to take the city through a campaign of attacks and bombardments that continued for almost three years, she began to succumb to the enemy's silent weapon—starvation. Once, she awoke lying beside a row of corpses. She had passed out in the street and been mistaken for dead. She went in search of her husband and found him in the hospital, recovering from his wounds. Seeing how thin she was, he secretly gave her his food during her daily visits until doctors caught him fainting and ordered him to stop. By war's end, the couple's home in Leningrad had been destroyed, and they had lost two children: one during infancy, and the other from diphtheria, a respiratory disease that killed thousands of Leningrad children.

Maria was 41 when she gave birth to her son, Vladimir, on October 1, 1952. She secretly baptized him in the Russian Orthodox faith, even keeping it from her husband because he was the secretary of the local Communist Party organization. In the Soviet Union, religious practices were officially forbidden.

## THE CREATION OF THE SOVIET UNION

Vladimir Putin was part of only the second generation to have been born in the Soviet Union. Created in 1922, it eventually

Photographed with his St. Petersburg school class in 1961, nine-year-old Vladimir Putin sits on the teacher's right.

consisted of 15 Soviet Socialist republics, including Russia. Russia was the centerpiece of the Soviet Union, politically because it contained the Kremlin, the seat of Soviet power, and geographically because it comprised three-fourths of the Soviet Union's territory. The borders of Russia reach Norway, Finland, Estonia, and Latvia to the northwest; Belarus and Ukraine to the west; Georgia, Azerbaijan, and Kazakhstan to the southwest; and China, Mongolia, and Korea to the southeast, making it the largest country in the world. Although rich in natural resources—especially oil, gas, and timber—Russia is generally dry and unsuited for agriculture. For centuries, under various royal families, overlords, and landowners, Russian peasants scratched out a living in hamlets where pigs and garden plots supported them.

The Communist-supported Russian Revolution came in 1917, deposing (and executing) the royal family of Tsar

Nicholas II. Within eight months, four governments had come and gone. In late summer 1917, an official named Alexander Kerensky seized power, proclaimed a democratic republic, and set a date for elections. The vote for the Constituent Assembly was Russia's first free national election. The new government produced the Declaration of the Rights of Toiling and Exploited Peoples, in which the assembly embraced the "fundamental task [of] the suppression of all forms of exploitation of man by man and the complete abolition of class distinctions in society. It aims to crush unmercifully the exploiter, to reorganize society on a socialistic basis, and to bring about the triumph of Socialism throughout the world."

It was not long, however, before the aims of this vision were twisted into an excuse for enforcing a new kind of oppression by an authoritarian state.

## LIFE UNDER STALIN'S REGIME

In the late 1920s, Joseph Stalin used political infighting to emerge as general secretary of the Communist Party of the Soviet Union. Until his death almost 30 years later, he held complete control over Soviet domestic and international policy. For the people of Russia, Stalin was the incarnation of heroism, the ideal of patriotism. "For Stalin—for our country!" roared the Soviet army when it attacked German invaders.

Yet beneath the exterior of "Uncle Joe," as Americans came to call Stalin during World War II, was a tyrant. Through mass arrests, deportations to prison camps, executions, and assassinations, Stalin ruled Russia and the Soviet Union in a climate of abject fear. Under him, the people chased after any comforts the government handed out—decent living quarters, extra food, jobs, special privileges, or positions of status within the Communist Party. The Putins were more fortunate than many. They benefited from the state's "generosity" in several ways, perhaps because young Vladimir's grandfather had been a cook at one of Stalin's country homes.

Leningrad, the city where the Putin family lived, had once been called St. Petersburg. Established in 1703 by Peter the Great as the capital of the Russian Empire, the city was called Petrograd during World War I. It was renamed Leningrad after 1924, in honor of Vladimir Ilyich Lenin, the leader of the Russian Revolution. (In 1991, as the result of a city referendum, the city was renamed St. Petersburg.) Under the tsars, or Russian emperors, St. Petersburg was Russia's cultural, intellectual, commercial, financial, and industrial center. After the capital was moved to Moscow in 1918, the city's importance declined, but it remained a cultural, scientific, and military-industrial center. When Putin grew up there in the 1950s, it still retained some of its former glory, but beneath was a layer of grime and neglect.

Putin's father was a toolmaker in a train-car factory and well paid by Soviet standards, which permitted the Putins to live in a tiny apartment that they shared with other families. To supplement the family income, Maria took various jobs. She worked as a janitor, made night deliveries for a bakery, and washed test tubes for a laboratory. Still, according to one of Putin's former teachers, Vera Dmitrievna Gurevich, the fifth-floor, 12-by-15-foot room where the Putins lived on Baskov Lane in the center of the city was dreadful.

"They had a horrid apartment," she said in Putin's biography. "It was communal, without any conveniences. There was no hot water, no bathtub. The toilet was horrendous. It ran smack up against a stair landing. And it was so cold—just awful—and the stairway had a freezing metal handrail. The stairs weren't safe either—there were gaps everywhere. . . . There was practically no kitchen. It was just a square, dark hallway without windows. A gas burner stood on one side and a sink on the other. There was no room to move around."

Behind the kitchen lived a family of three. Next door was a middle-aged couple. Putin became friendly with an elderly

Jewish couple in the building who chanted the words of the Talmud on the Sabbath.

For excitement on dull days, there were always the rats that scrambled up and down the stairs and hallways of the building. "There were hordes of rats in the front entryway," Putin remembered in his biography. "My friends and I used to chase them around with sticks. Once I spotted a huge rat and pursued it down the hall until I drove it into a corner. It had nowhere to run. Suddenly it lashed around and threw itself at me. I was surprised and frightened. Now the rat was chasing me. It jumped across the landing and down the stairs. Luckily, I was a little faster and I managed to slam the door shut in its nose."

## EDUCATION

When he started school, Putin did well. In the ninth grade, he was selected to attend Leningrad School No. 281, a school for the city's brightest students. Although the school specialized in science, Putin soon found that he was also drawn to the liberal arts such as literature, history, and art. Besides being a training ground for top students, the school was unusual in another way: Teachers used the underground samizdat (material that was photocopied and distributed hand to hand) in literature classes and questioned whether the promise of the Soviet state was realistic.

Putin's classmates and teachers remembered him as a top student who was self-confident, but also as someone who did not try to draw attention to himself. Smaller than others his age, at 11 he began to study judo and sambo, a Russian sport that is a cross between judo and wrestling. "Judo," Putin said to CNN.com, "is not just a sport, but a philosophy." It was not long before he had to put this "philosophy" into action.

One day, while the teacher's back was turned, a classmate gave Putin a good hard kick. Putin kicked back. After school, the bully and his friends were waiting. Putin calmly stepped

This 1969 photo shows Putin in the ninth grade, dancing with a girl named Elena.

forward, and with a few moves, brought down the bigger boy. He never boasted about it, but no one at school picked on him again. Years later, as president, when he was defending the conduct of the Russian war in Chechnya, Putin seemed to be drawing on the philosophy of his schoolyard days. *New York Times* reporter Celestine Bohlen quoted him as saying, "Only one thing can be effective in such circumstances: to go on the offensive. You must hit first and hit so hard that your opponent will not rise to his feet."

### FIRST STEPS TOWARD BECOMING A SPY

Even though he described himself in an article by Richard Beeston in *The Times* (of London) as "a hooligan" and a "real ruffian" as a teenager, at that time, Putin was already thinking seriously about his future. The movie that he saw

His high school training in judo no doubt helped prepare Putin (bottom) for his future life as a spy.

about the Soviet spy gave Putin an urge to read every novel he could find about espionage. Finally, he decided that the best course of action was to approach the KGB directly. He went to the Leningrad regional headquarters, approached the receptionist's desk, and explained that he wanted to know how to volunteer for the KGB.

"Some old guy came out and listened to me," Putin recalled. "I told him, 'I want to work for you.' 'I'm glad to hear that,' he said, 'but there are a few pointers I have to give you. First, initiative is not enough here. You have to either serve in the army or get a higher education.'"

"What's the best degree to get?" the young Putin asked, according to CNN.com. "A law degree," the KGB man replied.

"I understand," said Putin. He made up his mind to apply to the elite law school at Leningrad State University.

Later, at his judo class, Putin proudly informed his instructor of his plan. But his coach, aware of the KGB's reputation for suppressing dissent and making secret arrests, was less than impressed. Bernard Gwertzman of the *New York Times* wrote that the coach exclaimed, "What?! To catch people? What are you doing? You'll be a cop."

The coach's reaction did nothing to deter Putin. He saw espionage as a career that combined patriotism with courage and intelligence. His mind was made up, and friends who knew him well also knew that he tended to be headstrong about personal goals. "No one could stop me," Putin later said in his biography.

# CHAPTER

# 4

# On the Front Lines of the Cold War

BY ENROLLING IN LENINGRAD STATE UNIVERSITY IN 1970, PUTIN positioned himself perfectly as a potential candidate for the KGB. Aleksandr Lebedev, a former intelligence officer and the head of the Russian National Reserve Bank, described KGB recruits in those days in the *New York Times Magazine*: "They came out of the best places—Moscow State, Leningrad State, the Moscow State Institute for Foreign Relations. The state was looking for people with a talent to make others feel well disposed toward them. Tennis was encouraged, so you could move easily in high society in the West."

Putin may not have been a tennis player (tennis would have been a peculiar hobby for a young man from a working-class neighborhood), but his skills as a martial artist brought him honors. During his junior year at Leningrad State, he won

36

the Master of Sport in sambo—the top award—and he won it again two years later.

Not much is known about Putin in his college years. He seems to have devoted his time to studying. Judging from remarks made by one of his friends, Sergei Roldugin, Putin began to demonstrate the kind of coolness expected of someone interested in undercover work. Raldugin, a cello soloist at the performing theaters in St. Petersburg, lived in a world where music, self-expression, and art were important. At times, Putin's stoical behavior and shoulder-shrugging attitude got on his nerves.

"In principle he is a very emotional man," Raldugin recalled in a March 2000 article in *The Times* (of London), "but he was completely incapable of expressing his emotions. I used to say to him: 'Vovka [a nickname], it's frightening talking to you.' He is much better than he used to be. I am an actor, and I was trying to help as such. He had powerful emotions, but couldn't put them into words."

No amount of persuasion could convince the young pre-law student to drop the unsmiling expression he wore in public. Sometimes during conversations, his unblinking, ice-blue eyes made friends feel uncomfortable.

## LIFE-CHANGING EVENTS

Putin's mastery of his emotions could not control events around him, however. Two incidents stripped off the veneer of his outward aloofness—a car accident and a failed love affair.

During his junior year, his mother won the state-run lottery. It was a fantastic stroke of luck for the Putins, who, like most Soviet families, were constantly strapped for cash. Putin had so little money that he had just purchased his "first real coat" to wear in the harsh Russian winters. As the lottery winner, Maria could either take cash for the ticket or receive a new car. She chose the car, but promptly turned over the keys to her only son. Vladimir, the poor college student, was now the proud owner of an automobile fresh off the factory floor. "I was a reckless driver," *The Times* (of London) quoted him as saying, "but I was also frightened of crashing the car."

What happened was even worse than Putin's fear. One day, while cruising around Leningrad, he hit a pedestrian. "It wasn't my fault, it was proven," he said during an interview. "He was trying to kill himself. A real idiot. He ran away straight after the accident . . . I just got out of the car." Regardless of who was to blame, the accident shook up Putin. The KGB would only be interested in someone with a spotless record. One incident of criminal conduct or even poor judgment would take him out of the running.

A failed love affair proved to be another kind of problem for Putin. The girl Putin loved was a medical student, his first real love. In *The Times*, Raldugin recalled liking her: "She was a good person . . . strong-willed. She looked after him." As the law required, the pair filed an application for marriage, then both sets of parents bought rings, suits, and dresses—all that they could afford for the young couple's wedding day. Then, suddenly, Putin knew that marriage was not what he wanted. According to *The Times*, he said, "It was one of the most difficult decisions in my life. Very hard. But I had decided it was better to do it then than for both of us to suffer afterwards. I told her the whole truth, everything I thought I had to." When an interviewer later asked him to explain what changed his mind about marriage, Putin said he preferred not to talk about it.

### THE KGB RECRUIT

His academic life, unlike his personal life, bent to his will and self-discipline. Emotion had little to do with test scores and grades. In 1975, as he prepared to graduate from Leningrad State University law school, the KGB not only took notice of him, but actively recruited him. It was an honor. He was the only one chosen out of 100 applicants in his class. Valery

Golubev, who later served with Putin in the KGB in the early 1980s, recalled in the *New York Times Magazine*, "In the 1970s, when we joined, the choice of officers was exclusively of a high order. The state had the possibility to find and attract into that kind of work the most able, the most sincere, the most decent and the most ambitious of young people."

With no hesitation, Putin accepted the KGB's offer of an entry-level position in the First Chief Directorate, the foreign intelligence office. At last, his dream had been realized. He happily anticipated that he was going to live the life of the spy in the movie he had seen when he was a young man. He would serve his country by putting himself in risky situations that would bring him face-to-face with the motherland's enemies. He would outsmart those enemies to give his country the edge.

Putin was the perfect young recruit—he was well educated and well informed, and his ability to keep his emotions in check made him a good fit. KGB officers were expert at exerting psychological pressure. Felix Svetov, a writer who spent time in Stalin's prison camps as a child and who lost his father in the purges (the elimination of people the government deemed "undesirable"), said, "If the snow is falling, they will calmly tell you, the sun is shining." In fact, the only flaw that cropped up during Putin's initial KGB assessment was that he demonstrated a "lowered sense of danger," according to *The Times*, which Putin interpreted to mean that he responded too slowly to a threat.

## THE LIFE OF A SPY

Almost immediately, Putin began to slip into a spy's shadowy world of half-truths. One day, he bumped into two former high school classmates, Sergei and Yelena Kudrov. They asked him how he was and what he was doing. He answered vaguely that he was doing some work for the local prosecutor's office. The *Los Angeles Times* reported that to discourage further questions,

This photo shows a building of the former KGB at the Lyubanka Square in downtown Moscow. Although technically it no longer exists, many Russians still refer to the secret police as KGB.

Putin joked, "Before lunch, we're busy catching criminals. After lunch, we're busy shooting them." After some more small talk, he bid them a friendly good-bye and was off.

To test the new recruit, the KBG assigned Putin a routine task: to spy on foreigners in his hometown. The task had several purposes. It would provide newly minted spies with practical experience in picking people's brains for information, it would keep tabs on strangers and their whereabouts, and it would sound foreigners out on their ideas. If the foreigners appeared to pose a threat for any reason, they could be detained and briskly expelled from the country. Amy Knight, an American writing in the *Wilson Quarterly* magazine, a foreign affairs publication, described what it was like to encounter someone like Putin during her return to Leningrad in 1981 after having visited as a student in 1967:

> Fourteen years had not changed the rule: Forging acquaintances with local Russians was strictly out of bounds. Foreigners, especially Russian speakers like me, were still cordoned off from contacts with ordinary Russians by the efficient operations of Intourist and the infamous *dezhurnye*, the elderly ladies who were positioned on every hotel floor to monitor the comings and goings of guests. So it was very odd when an unusually friendly Russian man approached me as I sat in the lobby of my hotel, right under the watchful eyes of Intourist, and began earnestly telling me about the woes of Soviet life and expressing sympathy for American ideals. It took a while before I realized what was going on. I was the target of an entrapment effort. Shaken, I quickly broke off the conversation and hurried away.
>
> My new "acquaintance" was doubtless an employee of the local branch of the KGB. Part of his job was to hang around hotels spying on visiting foreigners and trying to single out a few—as in my case, apparently—who could be more directly exploited. This was the kind of elevated activity Vladimir

Putin did during the nine years he worked for the Leningrad KGB, from 1975 to 1984. (For all I know, the man in the Hotel Moskva's lobby may have been Putin, who has been aptly described as "professionally nondescript.") It is hard to imagine what people like Putin felt when they went through daily routines such as this, but I will never forget my own reaction. I felt like going up to my room and taking a long shower.

Although the work—duping foreigners into getting into trouble with the police—might be distasteful to most Americans, it was so much a part of the fabric of Soviet life that Putin never regretted his role. The *New York Times* reported that Putin said, "To be honest, I didn't think about it at all. Not one bit . . . My notion of the KGB came from romantic spy stories. I was a pure and utterly successful product of Soviet patriotic education."

## A PROMOTION AND A ROMANCE

He performed well during those years, and, in 1984, he was promoted to a year of study at the KGB's Red Banner Institute of Intelligence in Moscow. In the meantime, however, his personal life had taken a serious romantic turn again.

Putin's friend Sergei Roldugin had met a flight attendant from Kaliningrad. Roldugin was eager to show off his new Zhiguli—the first car he had ever owned—and offered to take her to a concert at the Lensoviet Theater. She agreed but also invited another flight attendant, Lyudmila. Roldugin gallantly arranged for a date for Lyudmila, too—his friend Vladimir.

On the day of the concert, Putin was nowhere in sight. Roldugin struggled to chat with two girls he hardly knew. In a *Times* (of London) article, he remembered, "They sat in my Zhiguli. We waited for him. I was incredibly embarrassed sitting there with them like that: various friends were going by, recognizing me—it wasn't at all how it should be. We sat like that for about an hour. All that time I was exhausting those

Putin and his wife, Lyudmila, pose in front of the Taj Mahal in India on October 4, 2000.

two girls with my conversation. At least that's how it seemed to me, but actually, we were all getting on fine. At last Volodya [a nickname for Putin] appeared. He was almost always late. We went to the theatre."

*The Times* also said that Lyudmila was not impressed with her blind date. "He was modestly, even poorly, dressed. He was inconspicuous—on the street I would have paid no attention to him." During the intermission, she tried to liven up the date with jokes, but Putin acted glum. At the end of the concert, though, the two couples agreed to go to another theater the next day. On the third day, they went out again.

It turned out that the somber and poorly dressed young man was somehow able to get tickets to any show in Leningrad. Lyudmila asked him what he did for a living. Putin said he was in "criminal investigations." Later, Roldugin was astonished when they took the girls to the train and Putin gave Lyudmila his address and phone number. It was so uncharacteristic of him that, as Lyudmila walked away, according to *The Times*, she heard Roldugin exclaim in mock surprise, "What? Have you gone mad?"

For three to four months, Lyudmila and Putin carried on a long-distance friendship. When she flew in to Leningrad, they went out on dates. All the while, she was not sure how she felt about her low-key boyfriend. At some point, however, she decided that his "inner strength" took time to understand. She was in love with him. They continued courting for three and a half years.

*The Times* reported a conversation that took place one evening at Putin's house. He said to her, "My little friend, you know now what kind of person I am. I'm not very easy-going." As he continued to list his shortcomings, it took Lyudmila a while to realize that he was proposing. Trying to help, she offered, "I've worked everything out."

"Well, if that's how things are," he said, "then I love you and I propose that we get married . . ." They were married three months later in a floating restaurant moored to a riverbank. In the 1983 wedding photos, Putin has a serious, businesslike expression on his face.

## AN IMPORTANT POST IN EAST GERMANY

Posted to the Red Banner Institute the following year, Putin prepared for what would inevitably be an important assignment outside Russia. He had encouraged Lyudmila to continue her education, and she completed a teaching degree in Spanish, French, and beginning Portuguese. Her skill in languages turned out to be an asset.

When Putin finally got his assignment, it was on the front lines of the Cold War—East Germany. Right before they left, the couple's first daughter, Masha, was born. Roldugin remembered in *The Times* how they all celebrated: "I had a relative with a [country cottage] near Vyborg, a great place, and we went there after they let [Lyudmila] out of the maternity ward and we all lived there together: [Putin], Lyuda, me and my wife. Of course we celebrated the birth of Masha. In the evenings we arranged dances—[Putin] was a real mover."

At age 32, Putin arrived in Dresden, East Germany, a prestigious post for a rising KBG officer. The German Democratic Republic of East Germany was home to 380,000 Soviet troops protected by intermediate-range missiles. Berlin was a constant source of Cold War tensions and intrigue. At the time, several thousand KGB officers reported to a headquarters at Karlshorst, outside Berlin. There, East German spymaster Marcus Wolf directed a sort of finishing school for young intelligence officers.

The biggest intelligence operation was the East German secret police, the Stasi, which monitored hundreds of thousands of citizens and kept millions of documents on file. The Stasi poked into every aspect of life—recording people's conversations, movements, even financial transactions—all to protect the state and advance its interests. It is estimated that by 1988, when Putin was in East Germany, the Stasi had more than 90,000 employees and some 170,000 collaborators. In other words, at least 1 out of every 50 East German adults was directly connected with the secret police. In Dresden alone, the information the Stasi kept on citizens, now preserved for historical research, stretches nearly seven miles in the archives.

Putin's office at No. 4 Angelikastrasse was the KGB's outpost directly across the street from the city's main Stasi headquarters. An important part of his job was to monitor East German attitudes and contacts with West Germans. Code-named Operation LUCH, the work also involved recruiting and preparing agents as informers. The *New York Times* wrote that Putin once commented matter-of-factly, "Agents work in the interests of the state," and added that "90 percent" of all intelli-

## THE *NEW YORK TIMES* WROTE THAT VLADIMIR PUTIN ONCE COMMENTED MATTER-OF-FACTLY, "AGENTS WORK IN THE INTERESTS OF THE STATE."

gence was collected with the collaboration of ordinary citizens. Putin was also responsible for "German-Soviet friendship," which probably meant he worked as a *zampolit*, a political officer who kept track of the loyalty of Soviet troops.

These jobs were just sidelines, however—necessary tasks that had to be carried out at the place where the Soviet Union bordered the West. The real spying to be done, which involved Putin deeply, was trying to steal technology secrets.

### THE CHANGING COLD WAR

By the mid-1980s, it was clear that the Soviet Union was beginning to lose the Cold War. In the 1950s, the contest had been over troop strength—a competition left over from World War II. In the 1960s, the game shifted to nuclear attack capability. In the 1970s, the United States seemed to accept the presence of Communism as a continuing challenge, and an East-West stalemate dragged on. In the 1980s, however, with the advent of miniaturized technology, the door opened to a whole new landscape of research and defense possibilities. The Soviet Union found itself mired in tanks, missiles, submarines—all the equipment of the old Cold War. The future lay with telecommunications, precision manufacturing, and biotechnology. Although the Soviet Union could boast that it had a 100 percent literacy rate among its citizens, far higher than in the United States, and that Russian medical, mathematical, scientific, and space and aviation research was very advanced, the Soviet bloc was far behind the West in computer-aided technology.

The issue came to light in May 1984, when chief of the Soviet general staff Marshal Nikolai Ogarkov publicly warned that the West's military high technology was outpacing that of the Soviet Union. At the Stasi headquarters across the street from Putin's offices, agents often preferred to work on a Western-made Commodore personal computer rather than on their own office mainframe.

## TRYING TO STEAL WESTERN TECHNOLOGY

Dresden, East Germany, became one of the focal points of Soviet hopes. There, the Soviets hoped to use intelligence operations to gain the technical knowledge they desperately needed to catch up with the West. The city was one of only five in the Soviet bloc with a microelectronics industry. It was home to the Robotron company, the Eastern bloc's largest mainframe computer maker and a microchip research center. Robotron provided the real jumping-off point for Putin's work in Dresden. Working hand in hand with the Stasi's foreign section, Putin's unit used contacts between Robotron and companies that included Siemens and IBM to acquire high technology for Moscow. It was one of the most important operations of the KGB.

Several times, Putin went to the Soviet embassy in Bonn, West Germany, and to West Berlin on a diplomatic passport as "Mr. Adamov" to meet with technicians who worked undercover for the Soviets. Once his picture was secretly snapped outside a department store while he apparently was waiting to meet a contact. Putin was good at his job—a trusted agent in a sensitive position—and in 1987, he received a bronze medal for his work with the Stasi.

Still, attempts by Putin and other KGB operatives were moving too slowly. It was very difficult to steal the complicated and rapidly evolving technology that was powering the West's widening lead in high technology. Moreover, diagrams of even the most classified technology meant nothing when the Soviets had no money to make copies of the West's hardware.

## PERESTROIKA AND GLASNOST

In 1987, the year Putin received his bronze medal, a new directive came from Moscow that was an enormous gamble: perestroika. Officially, perestroika was defined in many ways, but the essence of it was that the Soviet government was taking a fresh look at democracy and at encouraging individual creativity. Over the decades, state-ordered plans for everything from agriculture to education had crushed ingenuity, with disastrous effects on the economy. Through perestroika, Moscow was saying, in effect, "Who's got a good idea?" The second part of perestroika involved glasnost: open discussions with the West regarding social problems and policies.

In the space of only a few months, Putin's mission changed dramatically. Now he and his KGB colleagues would be helping to fix the collapsing Soviet economy, instead of outfoxing the motherland's enemies. In particular, they needed to put money outside the Soviet Union, where it could be tucked away safely in foreign banks, invested, and used to fund new ventures. It was spy work of another kind. Some journalists have said it was nothing more than large-scale money laundering—trying to keep funds hidden so they could be used for other purposes.

## A MOVE BACK TO ST. PETERSBURG

In any case, when the Berlin Wall fell in November 1989, the high-stakes spy game between the East and the West slowed to a crawl. Putin's practical background in law and economics was now more valuable to him and his superiors than his desire to live a romantic cloak-and-dagger life. The KGB brought him back to Russia.

In 1990, he returned to Leningrad, soon to be renamed St. Petersburg, accompanied by his wife, his daughter Masha, and a second daughter, Katya. He might have pushed for a higher post, somewhere inside the Kremlin, but he did not want to move to Moscow. "I have two small children and old parents," he later told journalist Natalya Nikiforova. "They are over 80, and we all live together. They survived the blockade during [World War II]. How could I take them from the place they were born in? I could not abandon them."

St. Petersburg, the city where he had spent his entire childhood and young adulthood, met and married his wife, and made the dreams of his youth come true, probably exerted an emotional pull on him. "Petersburg isn't Moscow; it's a European city," observed Valery Golubey, a longtime friend of Putin's, in a *New York Times Magazine* article.

> Every stone breathes these traditions, and it gets into the head of every Petersburger. Moscow is more Asiatic in its mentality, and the other regions are even more so. The people from Petersburg are more interesting, freer in their thoughts.

In addition, there were practical aspects for Putin to consider. He knew influential people in St. Petersburg. It might be good for his career, he decided, to pursue a graduate degree in international private law at his alma mater, Leningrad State University.

Vladimir and Lyudmila Putin, like millions of other Russians who could not remember a time when there was no Cold War, faced a future that seemed dark and uncertain. Going home to St. Petersburg at least offered the comfort of being in a familiar place.

CHAPTER

# 5

# "The Gray Cardinal" in St. Petersburg

THE SOVIET UNION DISSOLVED ON DECEMBER 26, 1991. THE NEXT DAY, Russia took the seat formerly held by the Soviet Union in the United Nations Security Council. The Communist bloc, which had once encircled two-thirds of the globe and stretched across 11 time zones, disappeared overnight.

Immediately, what was once Russia's strength—its giant military—became its heaviest financial burden. In earlier years, when satellite nations helped bear the costs of maintaining the Soviet war machine, Russia's factories had poured out a torrent of defense products. In fact, about 70 percent of the former Soviet Union's defense industries were located inside what became the Russian Federation. Now, a large number of state-owned defense businesses were on the brink of collapse because of cuts in orders for weapons.

## RUSSIA STRUGGLES TO COPE WITH CHANGE

In a real way, Russia was left holding the bag at the end of decades of headlong military expansion. To have defense industries switch to making civilian goods would have been the best course of action, but there was neither the investment money nor the markets for those goods yet. To make matters worse, Russia's tax system had such ridiculously high rates that although some firms struggled to pay, others defiantly refused to pay taxes at all. On the street, among the people, the underground economy of bartering was growing fast. Trading a pound of butter for a hammer, for instance, not only filled the need for hard-to-find goods, but spared the buyer and seller from having to pay taxes.

As the government scrambled to find ways to convert the state-controlled economy into a free-market economy, it became obvious that a certain class of professionals was desperately needed: those who understood the mysteries of how to generally create a favorable business climate.

Having come back to Russia with his family, Putin settled down to a humdrum life in St. Petersburg. The job the KGB assigned him could not have been duller. He was spying on foreign students at Leningrad State University, "a KGB officer under the roof, as we say," he later said in an article by Chris Treadaway, adding that the university's administration knew about it. It was a big step backward in his career, a steep comedown from the exciting days he had known in Dresden. With the national government floundering in Moscow, Putin had to wonder whom he was serving and what his mission was.

He endured his job at the university for a year and a half. Then, in 1991, he resigned. His rank after 16 years of service was lieutenant colonel. Leaving the KGB was a wrenching experience for Putin. In a bureau at home, he stashed his old Communist identification cards and other documents. Celestine Bohlen of the *New York Times* wrote that, before he shut the drawer, he "made the sign of the cross over them," as if laying that part of his life to rest.

## A JOB FOR PUTIN IN POLITICS

Although Putin would continue to rely on his KGB connections throughout his career, he was hungry for a new assignment, a new opportunity of some kind. It was not long in coming.

Putin ran into his former economic law professor, Anatoly Sobchak. Sobchak had become a leader in the first wave of democratic reformers—outspoken critics of the old Soviet system who were now eager for the political and economic revolution they had long awaited. As the elected chairman of the city council, Sobchak was on the lookout for bright, like-minded people to assist him. In Putin, a former student he knew well, he saw exactly the sort of person—someone who was knowledgeable about Western-style democracy—he needed on his team. Besides, he must have known Putin's reputation for being cool under pressure, another asset in the tough fight ahead. After all, there were many people in Russia who saw patriotism and Communism as identical. For them, democracy was irresponsible and unrealistic. The reformers knew it could take a generation, or even longer, to erase the last traces of the old ways.

The two men talked at length. Putin, always interested in politics, recognized that Sobchak and others like him represented the new order. The past was gone, and anyone who was smart had to make a move now. Putin did not need much convincing. He made an appointment to see his academic advisor at Leningrad State and dropped his plans for proceeding with a graduate degree. Instead, he told his advisor, he was going to work as an aide for Councilman Sobchak. (Some sources say that Putin left the KGB after, not before, he met Sobchak because his KGB ties would look improper.) "Vladimir clearly realized we couldn't double-deal, we couldn't play a double game," said Valery A. Golubev, a former KGB agent and Sobchak staff member who quit the spy agency at the same time, in the *Los Angeles Times*.

This 1994 photo shows Putin during the election for the NDR Party in St. Petersburg.

Putin was lucky that he got involved with Sobchak when he did. Soon, the system of city government was changed, and Sobchak became St. Petersburg's first post-Soviet elected mayor. He had his work cut out for him, and his job was made harder by his own shortcomings. Sobchak, like many early democrats, had almost no experience in elected office and "was not prepared to govern," according to journalist Sergei Shelin of *New Times* magazine. He constantly fought with members of the newly renamed legislature, the city Duma. Many times, Sobchak sent Putin to the deputies on errands of peace, recalled Mikhail Amosov, a member of the Yabloko Party, in the *Washington Post*. "Sobchak had bad relations with the lawmakers.

There were always frictions. Sobchak always wanted to put them in their place; he treated them like an enemy force."

## THE AUGUST COUP

Just a few months after Putin signed on with Sobchak, his first real test of loyalty arrived. In August 1991, Soviet hard-liners mounted a coup attempt against President Mikhail Gorbachev. Later dubbed the August Coup, a self-appointed eight-man Committee of the State of Emergency detained Gorbachev outside Moscow and attempted to seize the government.

Sobchak happened to be in Moscow when fighting started between troops and citizens. He publicly vowed to fight the overthrow. He flew back to St. Petersburg, ignoring the possibility that anti-democracy plotters might be waiting to ambush him when he arrived. Putin met his boss at the airport with an armed security force. During the next few days, while the rebellion continued, Putin successfully persuaded the anti-Gorbachev forces in Moscow to keep military troops out of St. Petersburg. The August Coup failed, largely due to future Russian president Boris Yeltsin's leadership. Sobchak and his administration had supported the winning side.

## PUTIN GETS A PROMOTION

Putin, the former mayor's aide, was quickly promoted to chairman of the Committee for External Relations—an impressive-sounding title that meant he was supposed to encourage foreign investment in St. Petersburg. The city had been intended to be a "window to Europe" when it was built by Tsar Peter the Great, and Putin proceeded in that spirit. Using the excellent skills in the German language that he had acquired in Dresden, he was able to woo German banks to the city, including the multinational BNP-Dresdner Bank. He also set up a legitimate currency exchange—a necessary step to attract tourists and businesspeople—and he put the hotels that had been run by the state under private ownership.

In August 1991, Communist hard-liners, who disagreed with the new direction being taken in Russian politics, staged a coup to overthrow President Mikhail Gorbachev. During the so-called August Coup, Russian citizens fought military troops on the streets of Moscow.

Not everyone approved of his enthusiasm for Westernizing the city, however. "All the work we did on privatization was supported by Putin, and not everyone was for it," recalled Sergei Belyaev, a former deputy mayor and later a member of the Russian parliament. Old-style Communists, in particular, who wished for a return to the days of centralized government, watched the efforts of Sobchak's young protégé with suspicion, even contempt.

In addition to political opposition, Putin also had the media and special-interest groups to contend with. It would not help his efforts to have critical newspaper editors or broadcasters undermine his work. In fact, his dislike of a free press would grow over the years until, when he became president, he actively tried to suppress dissent.

Among the city's deal-makers, however, Putin became known as the man to see if something needed to get done. In negotiations with people, his KGB past served him well. He tended to listen instead of talk, and he kept his emotions under tight rein. "When we worked in Putin's agency, we had 100 percent discipline and we had 100 percent order," said Marina Manevich, a former staff member, in the *Los Angeles Times*. "This was not coerced. It was introduced softly, tactfully and in a very intelligent manner."

Putin's somberness, his formality, and his ability to work effectively behind the scenes, earned him a nickname, the Gray Cardinal. Sobchak could not speak highly enough of him. In John Lloyd's article in the *New York Times Magazine*, he said, "He was utterly professional. He worked very well with others, knew how to talk to them. He was decisive. When you put something to him, he would think about and, if he could do it, he would say yes, never no. Judge his success—he was in charge of foreign investment, and by 1993 we had 6,000 joint ventures, half the total in Russia."

## CORRUPTION AND SCANDAL ROCK THE RUSSIAN GOVERNMENT

Although his influence in city government grew—Sobchak named him deputy mayor in 1994—publicly, Putin was careful to remain in the background. He avoided drawing attention to himself in these heady, early days of democracy.

Relations with the West had opened a floodgate of money, and with it came a surge of corruption that spread through

Russian society. Greedy hands grabbed at the humanitarian assistance that came from the U.S. government—billions of dollars in food and medical equipment, as well as supplies donated by American charities and the U.S. Defense Department. Russian bureaucrats became rich by double-dealing with the public, exploiting the weaknesses of "reform."

Putin took care to keep a low profile. His instincts as a former spy probably told him that he could be more effective by staying out of the public eye. "In the Petersburg days, it was always other people in front of the television cameras," said Igor Artemyev, leader of the Yabloko Party, in an article by Chris Treadaway. "Almost all the other vice mayors lined up next to the boss. Putin was always in the farthest corner."

Once, however, scandal did touch him. It happened early during his tenure in city government. *Washington Post* writer David Hoffman reported that Marina Salye, who was then a member of the legislature's food committee, recalled, "There was no food in the city at all. There was no money. Barter was the only way—say, metals for potatoes and meat."

Because St. Petersburg was a port and military city, the state-owned shipbuilding and defense factories were stocked with precious metals. Salye said contracts were signed to trade metals to Western countries for food, but she discovered that the metals had been sold at discount prices, that food prices were inflated, and that the food had never arrived. It turned out that phony companies had taken the profits and disappeared. Salye said she thought Putin "was manipulating these contracts and was directly involved. But it hasn't been proved." Salye confronted Putin, she recalled in the *Washington Post*, but he brushed off her inquiries. "Everything is correct," she said he told her. "You are just making up things." The deputies recommended that the mayor fire Putin, but Sobchak refused. The city prosecutor's office investigated and declined to press charges, citing a lack of evidence.

Although the administration of St. Petersburg Mayor Anatoly Sobchak (left) seemed to be rife with scandal, most sources believe that his right-hand man, Putin (right), was able to avoid corruption. Some people argue, however, that he simply avoided getting caught.

## POLITICAL SUCCESS AND FAILURE

Putin was developing the thick skin necessary to be involved in politics, and in autumn 1995, he accepted success and failure with equal composure. During Sobchak's frequent absences from St. Petersburg—while he was being groomed as a possible successor to then president Boris Yeltsin—Putin acted as mayor in his place. He was instrumental in getting the city budget passed by the legislature, no small feat for a newcomer to politics. His inexperience, however, tripped him up that autumn when he was running the local campaign for the NDR (Our Home: Russia) Party in St. Petersburg. Putin took heat for plastering thousands of expensive posters all over the city. "What could we do?" said Putin with a shrug, according to CNN.com. "Moscow sent too many portraits. We couldn't just waste them."

His boss, Sobchak, was not as good as Putin at letting criticism roll off his back. Rumors of scandal swirled around him and he lashed out at his enemies. (When Sobchak died of a heart attack in 2000 at the age of 62, he was still plagued by criminal charges of corruption. Putin spoke at his funeral and referred emotionally to his mentor as a man "hounded to his death" by enemies.) In 1996, Sobchak ran for re-election. He made Putin his campaign manager. The voters were tired of hearing about how the city council was often rocked by controversy or infighting. Sobchak lost, and when he stepped down as mayor, Deputy Mayor Putin resigned.

Putin's experiment in local politics had ended abruptly, but his loyalty and administrative skills had not gone unnoticed. Even as far away as Moscow, Putin had come to the attention of the power brokers in the Kremlin.

# 6

# To the Kremlin

**EVEN IF ANATOLY SOBCHAK HAD WON RE-ELECTION AS MAYOR OF** St. Petersburg, Putin's career might have taken a negative turn. Shortly after the election, Sobchak's political enemies pounced, accusing him of official corruption. Had Sobchak won the election, Putin, his right-hand man, would probably have been locked in a battle to defend himself and his boss.

The new mayor asked Putin to stay on in city government because of his ability and reputation. If he had accepted the offer, he might have faced charges that otherwise would have been directed at Sobchak, who eventually went into exile outside of Russia, beyond the reach of his frustrated enemies.

In any event, Putin's loyalty to his former economics professor, who had made it possible for him to enter politics, left him with no practical choice except to resign as deputy mayor.

## A NEW POST IN THE FEDERAL GOVERNMENT

It was wise that he did resign. At the Kremlin, Anatoly Chubais and Aleksei Kudrin, two former residents of St. Petersburg, helped get him a post inside the federal government. Chubais was at the height of his powers as a deputy prime minister. Kudrin held an important position in the finance ministry. They made the appropriate phone calls and pulled the right strings, and Putin, whose political career might have stalled in St. Petersburg without their help, was whisked away to Moscow.

The position he received in 1996 was as a deputy chief administrator—a fairly colorless job—but it put him at the heart of power in Russia. The administration he was joining, however, was in deep turmoil.

The scramble for money that Putin had witnessed in St. Petersburg's city government was magnified a hundred times in Moscow. Democracy was not coming quietly to Russia. Instead, a poisonous atmosphere had developed in which people seemed to care only about themselves. Semi-criminal financial magnates—the so-called oligarchs—were plundering the country with the help of corrupt officials in the Kremlin. The oligarchs' power, especially over banking and exports of raw materials—oil gas, coal, and timber—had cost the state billions in lost revenue. Under the guise of making reforms, powerful interests were holding up the emergence of a free-market economy and discouraging the foreign investment Russia so desperately needed. Michael Urban, a Soviet expert at the University of California at Santa Cruz, in an interview with Fiona Morgan of Salon.com, said that reform "is a code word that means absolutely nothing. They've had their reform. What it has produced is a small oligarchy of people who have stolen everything that was there to steal." At the top of the heap in the Kremlin were influence-peddlers known as "the Family"—an insider group allied, by blood or political ties, with the Russian president, Boris Yeltsin.

The bell tower of the Moscow Kremlin is shown in this photograph. The complex, which overlooks the Red Square, is the official residence and workplace of the president.

## THE GOVERNMENT OF BORIS YELTSIN

Yeltsin had won his power in the pro-democratic atmosphere of the late 1980s. His go-it-alone style and direct approach won him popular approval and, in 1989, a seat in the legislature. Yeltsin gained another electoral victory in 1991, becoming Russia's first freely elected leader. The chaotic months later that year saw the August Coup against Soviet president Mikhail Gorbachev, confusion at the head of the government, and the dissolution of the Soviet Union. "When the dust settled," wrote *Time* magazine, "Russia was independent, Gorbachev had retired, and Yeltsin was alone on center stage."

By the fall of 1993, Yeltsin was locked in a ongoing brawl with the Russian parliament, the Duma, which had blocked, overturned, or ignored his attempts to draft a new constitution, conduct new elections, and continue to make progress with democratic and economic reforms. To give himself leverage, Yeltsin had begun to surround himself with former KGB officials. He wanted their expertise in investigation and surveillance—not only to help him judge the political winds, but to get the advantage over his enemies.

In a dramatic speech in September 1993, Yeltsin dissolved the Duma and called for new national elections and a new constitution. The standoff between the executive branch and the legislature turned violent in October, when supporters of the Duma mounted an armed insurrection. Yeltsin ordered the army to respond with force to capture the parliament building. Television viewers worldwide watched as Russian tanks rolled up and sprayed the exterior of the building, called the White House, with heavy machine-gun fire.

Despite frequent challenges to his authority, Yeltsin remained Russia's dominant political figure. In December 1993, voters elected a new parliament and approved a new constitution drafted by the Yeltsin government. The new constitution gave the president considerable power; there is no vice president, and the legislative branch is far weaker than the executive. The president nominates the highest state officials, including the prime minister, who must be approved by the Duma. The president can pass decrees without consent from the Duma. He is also head of the armed forces and of the national security council.

Two years later, in 1995, voters elected to the Duma a broad array of parties, including ultranationalists, liberals, agrarians, and Communists. In the 1996 presidential election, Yeltsin was reelected in the second round following a spirited campaign. Both the presidential and parliamentary elections were judged generally free and fair by international observers.

## THE WAR IN CHECHNYA

Beyond the walls of the Kremlin, Russia is a federation, but the relationship between the central government and the regional and local authorities was vague during Yeltsin's administration, and it is still evolving today. The Russian Federation consists of 89 components, including the two federal cities of Moscow and St. Petersburg. The constitution clearly defines the federal government's exclusive powers, but it also leaves most key regional issues to be worked out by the federal government and the federation components.

As a result, when rebels in the southern Republic of Chechnya attempted to break away from Russia in late 1994, the federal government saw the revolt as a serious erosion of unity. The region, which lies between the Black Sea and Caspian Sea, is predominantly Muslim and has had a long history of anti-Russian unrest since the time of the tsars. This time, Yeltsin responded to the unrest with a brutal military operation.

"Russia feels itself pushed around. Its empire collapses," said Michael Urban of the University of California in his interview with Fiona Morgan. "The country itself, the Soviet Union, disintegrates. Russia thereafter is not taken seriously in international affairs . . . if there were a rebellion in East Los Angeles, and the U.S. Army went in there to stop it and failed,

Chechen rebels, including leader Aslan Maskhadov (wearing gray jacket) pose under the flag of an independent Chechnya in 1994. Russian officials blamed Maskhadov, who was killed in a 2005 raid, for the school hostage crisis.

and East L.A. became de facto independent, that would be the analogy with Chechnya. You can imagine how crazy people would be in this country." During the two-year war that followed, there were numerous violations of human rights on both sides. The Russian army used heavy weapons against Chechen people. Tens of thousands of civilians were killed and more than 500,000 were displaced during the war. The conflict, which received close attention in the media, raised serious human-rights concerns abroad as well as in Russia. In 1996, human-rights activist Sergey Kovalev resigned as chairman of the Presidential Human Rights Commission to protest the Russian government's record, particularly on the war in Chechnya. (In addition, prison conditions in Russia fell well below international standards. The year Kovalev resigned, according to human-rights groups, between 10,000 and 20,000 prisoners and detainees died, most because of overcrowding, disease, and lack of medical care.)

After numerous unsuccessful attempts to institute a cease-fire, in August 1996, the Russian and Chechen authorities negotiated a settlement that resulted in a complete withdrawal of Russian troops. When Putin began in his new post that year, the Russian people were dispirited and the government was disgraced. All the while, the plundering of valuable resources by the oligarchs continued.

## PUTIN BEGINS HIS NEW JOB

Nevertheless, Putin was, in some ways, a good fit with the Yeltsin administration. A former KBG agent, he was smart and well informed. Moreover, KGB officials had a reputation of being incorruptible, and Yeltsin needed to bolster his public relations in any way he could. Human-rights activists were wary of the growing list of former spies being brought to work in the Kremlin, but Yeltsin ignored their protests.

Putin's first job was as a deputy to Pavel Borodin, the Kremlin's business manager. Borodin reportedly controlled $600 billion in Russian government property and other assets. He was also at the center of several corruption scandals himself, including an alleged kickback scheme that involved the Swiss construction firm Mabetex. Mabetex won lucrative contracts to restore Kremlin buildings and may have paid credit-card bills for members of the Yeltsin "Family." Putin was assigned to a task similar to what he had been doing in Dresden at the end of the Cold War: pulling out Russia's assets from countries where its missions had closed. In other words, his job was to recoup as much of Russia's money as possible from former members of the Soviet Union.

During the same period, Putin found time to complete a postgraduate dissertation, which usually takes three years of study. He received a prestigious "candidate of science" degree, the equivalent of a Ph.D., from the Mining

Institute in St. Petersburg in June 1997, when he was also working in the Kremlin.

Earlier, at Leningrad State University, Putin had said that he wanted to research international private law, but his 218-page dissertation was about a completely different topic. The title was "Strategic Planning of the Renewal of the Minerals-Raw Materials Base of the Region in Conditions of the Formation of Market Relations." Much of the paper discussed the savings gained from building a port and roads in St. Petersburg. It offers little insight into Putin's views of the market economy. The Mining Institute refused to show Putin's thesis to a news reporter. When the reporter located a copy of a summary in the institute's library, officials snatched it away, saying it was private property.

## PUTIN MOVES UP IN THE YELTSIN GOVERNMENT

In March 1997, Yeltsin promoted Putin to deputy head of the presidential administration and head of the Main Oversight Department, which was responsible for seeing that Yeltsin's decrees were carried out. Putin's KGB training served him well here, too, according to the *Moscow Times* and other Russian newspapers. He assembled files on regional leaders so they could be pressured into following Yeltsin's policies. He also began to bring allies into the administration, including a fellow KGB veteran whom Putin selected to replace him when he was again promoted, to first deputy chief of staff in May 1998.

After only two months as first deputy, in July 1998, Yeltsin appointed Putin director of the Federal Security Service (FSB), which had replaced the dismantled KGB. During Putin's time at the agency, the FSB brought a number of environmental activists to court. Yeltsin also gave Putin and the FSB the job of "safeguarding" the upcoming Duma and presidential elections, a mission many Russian people believed was really to make sure that Yeltsin's allies were elected. In March 1999, Yeltsin named Putin to the post of secretary of the Russian Security Council, where he coordinated policy between the ministries of defense, FSB, foreign intelligence (SVR), interior, and others.

By this time, Yeltsin's health was failing, and so was his popularity. In his struggles with the Duma, he had appointed and fired five prime ministers in 17 months. So when on August 9, 1999, Yeltsin sacked Prime Minister Sergei Stepashin and appointed Putin to the post, most observers expected it to be another short-term appointment. Most Western analysts, according to the Canadian Broadcast Corporation, asked, "Who is Vladimir Putin?"

## PUTIN AS PRIME MINISTER

Then came a greater surprise: Yeltsin stated vigorously that he favored Putin as his successor to the presidency, an announcement that was generally met by most observers with skepticism or suspicion. In the *Los Angeles Times*, Moscow mayor Yurii Luzkov, a probable rival for the presidency, warned of shady dealings: "Making public the name of the preferred successor one year ahead of elections either means that Yeltsin has decided that all the power will go to an emergency organ and Putin would become, for instance, a dictator, without any presidential election."

Putin's response to Yeltsin's endorsement was characteristically low-key. "What will happen further and whether I will have the moral right to run for president will depend on what I can accomplish," he said in remarks on the floor of the Duma. (Putin's father, suffering from a heart condition, died shortly thereafter. The *New York Times Magazine* reported that he said on his death bed, "My son is like a tsar!" Putin's mother had died a year earlier from cancer.)

In the days after he was named as acting prime minister, 47-year-old Putin demonstrated that he would not be waiting for orders from Yeltsin. He expressed a willingness to quickly quash Islamic rebels who were battling Russian forces in the Caucasus and also said he favored rebuilding Russia's

Boris Yeltsin and Vladimir Putin meet in the Kremlin on December 27, 1999, shortly before Yeltsin announced his resignation.

security services, which were greatly weakened in the breakup of the Soviet Union. ABC News.com reported that his main task as prime minister, however, would be "improving the life of the people, the population's standard of living." But, then, as if he were following his own instincts, Putin went after Islamic rebels.

In response to incursions by Chechen Islamic militants into neighboring Dagestan, Putin ordered the Russian army to expel them. The war erupted fully again in October, after reports that Chechen separatists had bombed apartment buildings in Moscow and other Russian cities, resulting in 300 deaths. In the face of international protest of human rights violations against the fierce but militarily weak Chechens, Putin insisted that crushing the rebellion was a matter of national security. "We shall not allow the national pride of Russians to be trod upon," he said in an article by Stephen

Mulvey of BBC News. "We are sure of the power and prosperity of our country."

Putin's popularity soared to an incredibly high 60 percent approval rating in the polls. CNN reported, "Traumatized by apartment bombings in Moscow and other cities blamed on 'Chechen terrorists,' fed up with lawlessness and kidnappings in Chechnya, fueled by ethnic animosity toward Chechens, most Russians strongly supported the war, and still do."

The attack on Chechnya was labeled as "antiterrorist operations" by the Kremlin, which therefore required no parliamentary approval. The people overwhelmingly believed that order needed to be imposed in the region to enable overall stability within the country. Analyst Lilia Shevtsova of the Carnegie Center in Moscow wrote: "Chechnya . . . was a good excuse for consolidation, because it served simultaneously as an internal and external enemy."

The general belief then was that Putin could be trusted to do what needed to be done, and, after years of instability under Yeltsin, his decisiveness came as a relief.

## PUTIN BECOMES ACTING PRESIDENT

On New Year's Eve, 1999, Yeltsin went on television and dropped a bombshell. He announced he was stepping down and naming Putin acting president.

Vladimir Putin, who just eight years earlier had been a KGB lieutenant colonel spying on foreigners in St. Petersburg, had suddenly arrived on the world stage. Almost nobody knew who he was. He had been prime minister of Russia for only a few months, and less was known of him than of any Russian leader.

"We're scrambling," one American intelligence official told the *New York Times*. Even in his own country, Putin's career was shrouded in mystery. "Few people know who Putin is and what are his views about the economy of Russia," said Lilia Shevtsova, of the Carnegie Center. "We know all of his views about Chechnya, where he gained his absolutely amazing, sky-rocketing approval rating. But this is it."

The 2000 election was officially scheduled for June, six months away. Yeltsin and his allies, however, used their power to force the election to move up to March. With virtually no opponents facing him, and a campaign season shortened to only 12 weeks, Putin prepared for his first run for public office—that of president, the most powerful seat in the Russian Federation. On New Year's Day, he received a call from U.S. president Bill Clinton. The White House press secretary was quoted in the *National Review* as saying that Clinton expressed his belief that "they were off to a good start, and this was encouraging for the future of democracy in Russia."

Yeltsin had picked Putin in part because he didn't know how to deal with the new challenges facing the country. Yeltsin was not good at creating unity and using statesmanship. He felt Putin was a good unifier, and he also believed that Putin possessed the crucial combination of qualities to pull the country together in the coming century.

People saw in Vladimir Putin what they wanted to see: His KGB training allowed him to remain inscrutable. The mix of old and new that he created has resulted in an approval rating that has hovered around 70 percent for years. The Russian people longed for order, stability, and tranquility and he gave them a sense of that. They were tired of revolution and reforms that never seemed to make a difference in their lives. He seems to have successfully balanced the desires of the Communists who want to hold onto the old parliamentary authoritarianism with those of the new liberals who defend democracy.

# 7

# President of Russia

**BORIS YELTSIN'S ADMINISTRATION HAD BRIDGED THE TUMULTUOUS YEARS** between 1991 and 1999, which spanned the end of the Soviet Union and the first full decade of post-Cold War Russia. It had been almost 10 years of political battle. In 1991, Yeltsin's leadership had stopped the August Coup against his predecessor, Mikhail Gorbachev. As Russia's first democratically elected president, Yeltsin had to struggle constantly to keep the legislature from trying to control the executive branch. In the mid-1990s, the war in Chechnya had been a catastrophe until Prime Minister Putin rescued Russian pride. Behind all of these events, rumbling in the background, was the sound of the Russian economy collapsing and being cheered on by bitter Eastern Europeans who hated Russia. As *Time* magazine observed, "By the time of his resignation at the end of 1999, both Yeltsin and his country were in many ways shadows of their former formidable selves." Yeltsin stepped down on December 31,

Just after he announced his resignation on New Year's Eve in 1999, Boris Yeltsin shook the hand of his chosen successor, Vladimir Putin, in a symbolic ceremony at the Kremlin that showed the transfer of executive power.

1999, but not, like the old political warrior like he was, without protecting himself.

## YELTSIN USES HIS POWER TO HELP PUTIN

First, Yeltsin enormously increased Putin's chances of winning the presidential election by seeing to it that the vote was moved up from June to March. Although Putin was Yeltsin's handpicked successor, already very popular for the way he was handling the renewed war in Chechnya, it was possible that by June, the war might turn sour. The sooner the voting, the more likely Putin would sweep to victory. Moreover, cutting the campaign season in half would catch any of Putin's would-be opponents by surprise.

Next, Yeltsin may have looked out for his personal interests. It is possible that he made a pact with Putin, extracting a guarantee of immunity from prosecution. Some Kremlin-watchers believe Yeltsin wanted to guard the entire "Family"—his band of relatives and oligarchs who represented big money. "The election of a successor to Boris Yeltsin who could protect the interests of the former president, his family, and their closest allies among Russia's tycoons has been a paramount concern of those around Yeltsin," said the *National Review*. "It is almost unthinkable that [Putin] could have achieved his new post, which virtually assures his election to succeed Yeltsin in March, without cutting a deal with the Family." On the other hand, if Putin agreed not to touch the Family, "both ordinary Russians and Western investors will dismiss him as a weakling and a fake," said *Time*.

## ACTING PRESIDENT PUTIN AND HIS POLICIES

As though taking the middle road, Putin issued a flurry of personnel directives during the first week of January that seemed to balance one another. His first act as interim president declared that Yeltsin would be exempt from criminal or civil prosecution. Then, a few days later, he fired Yeltsin's daughter, Tatyana Dyachenko, from the Kremlin payroll. He also removed his former boss Pavel Borodin from the government properties office, assigning him to a lightweight diplomatic post instead. Borodin had controlled the largest assets in the Russian economy—$600 billion. For months, Swiss banking authorities had loudly alleged that Kremlin contractors had paid millions in bribes to Borodin's office to obtain government business. But Yeltsin had never lifted a finger in response. By dumping Borodin, Putin seemed to be signaling that he would be his own man. Still, he retained the services of Yeltsin's chief of staff and first deputy chief of staff, a reassurance that he was no radical, either. These mixed messages played well in the media.

Knowing how to walk a fine line, a skill bred into Putin by the KGB, had consistently helped him to rise through the ranks of power. He had emerged from the corruption-ridden city government of St. Petersburg without a scratch. Now he had done the same in the Yeltsin administration. Added to this, his integrity and loyalty were known to be as unshakable as his patriotism. "He's a decent, tough and energetic man who was out of public politics due to the specifics of his job," said Boris Nemtsov, a former deputy prime minister, in an article on ABC News.com. Though he tended to avoid the spotlight, he nonetheless knew how to act symbolically in the public eye when necessary. The *New York Times Magazine* described what happened at a ceremony in the Kremlin to celebrate the New Year. Putin came into the vast hall from one side to meet Aleksei II, the head of the Russian Orthodox Church, who entered from another. Putin knelt to kiss the patriarch's hands.

"Vladimir Vladimirovich," said the master of ceremonies to Putin as he rose, "what is your message for the new millennium?" "Love," said Putin.

Putin was clearly the man of the hour as the year 2000 began. Almost unopposed in the presidential race, amazingly popular in the polls, especially among younger Russians, and confident that he had the whole weight of the Yeltsin political machine behind him, Putin began to campaign.

## THE CAMPAIGN FOR PRESIDENT

To the Western world, Putin's dourness seemed to be at odds with the usual exuberance of politicians when they run for office. In fact, he barely bothered to hide how much he disliked the whole campaign process. In an article by Chris Treadaway, Putin said he found it distasteful. "One has to be insincere and promise something which you cannot fulfill," he said. "So you either have to be a fool who does not understand what you are promising, or deliberately be lying." He refused to publish a political platform, refused to debate, and said that campaign advertising was undignified: "good for selling Tampax and Snickers, he remarked recently," said *Time* magazine, "but not candidates for high office."

The Western media found that there was not much hard political news to cover. Russian insiders who might have had stories to tell about Putin were not eager to meet with journalists. The rumor was that those who spoke out would feel the wrath of his KGB connections. A small army of former friends, classmates, neighbors, and teachers, however, did approach reporters. They wanted their association with Putin to be known and appreciated. CNN's Moscow correspondent got so tired of hearing nostalgic stories about the young Vladimir Putin that she posted a sign on her door that read, "NO MORE PUTIN MEMOIRS!"

As the days rolled on toward election time, Putin seemed to enjoy being the stealth candidate. The newspaper *Kommersant Daily* asked him whether he would become a different person once he won the office of president in his own right: "Do you really have the desire to change all and everything?" According to the *Los Angeles Times*, Putin replied, "I won't tell you." As one member of the Russian parliament remarked on CNN.com, Putin was telling voters, "Elect me now and I'll tell you later who I am." Anyone who was curious enough to read about his background could find the official version in *First Person: An Astonishingly Frank Self-Portrait by Russia's President*, a campaign biography written by two Moscow journalists and a member of Putin's press department.

When he did speak on the record, usually at prearranged photo opportunities, he promised to distance himself from Yeltsin's cronies and to crack down on corruption—two themes that met with automatic approval. Experienced watchers of the Russian political scene were not so sure, though. Speaking

## CARNEGIE CENTER ANALYST LILIA SHEVTSOVA WARNED THAT PUTIN ULTIMATELY WAS "HOSTAGE OF THE REGIME THAT HE INHERITED."

to National Public Radio news, Carnegie Center analyst Lilia Shevtsova warned that Putin ultimately was "hostage of the regime that he inherited." She also suggested that Putin would try to consolidate power, and ignore "pivotal rules of the liberal democracy. He doesn't understand what a system of checks and balances is. He doesn't understand why we need free press, and why we need competitive elections."

### PUTIN WORKS TO REVIVE THE STRENGTH OF THE GOVERNMENT

In fact, since his first days as acting president, Putin had been quietly but steadily rebuilding, stone by stone, the strength of the Kremlin as the citadel of power in Russia. On January 5, after only five days in office, he clamped down on the Internet, turning it from a vehicle for self-expression into a monitoring device. By signing an amendment to the Law on Operational Investigations, Putin gave all police and security agencies the right to monitor, at will, the private e-mail correspondence of 2 million Internet users in Russia. The regulation required all Internet service providers to install a rerouting device that would connect the provider and all of its users to the headquarters of the FSB, the new version of the old KGB. Without obtaining a warrant, the police could go through people's e-mail, reading whatever they wanted.

In fact, 6 of Putin's first 12 decrees raised the specter of the old Soviet Union by emphasizing the power of the state. One reestablished mandatory training for military reservists. Another censored information about the war in Chechnya heavily. This reversed the earlier open news policy during the first Chechen war of 1994 to 1996. In late January, Putin's finance minister announced that defense spending would be increased by 50 percent.

Putin's goal was not to win the hearts and minds of people in the West, however. He needed the support of Russian voters as the March election drew near. He moved quickly to pay overdue wages and pensions. Then, a modest upturn in Russian economy added another boost to his campaign. The war in Chechnya continued to receive high marks from Russian citizens, and his sober, no-nonsense manner appealed to urban professionals. In answer to those who accused him of curtailing freedom of expression or appointing too many former KGB officials to high posts, Putin said dismissively in the *Los Angeles Times*, "This logic is characteristic of people with a totalitarian way of thinking. In theory, that's how a man should behave if he wants to stay in this place for the rest of his life. I don't."

## PUTIN OFFICIALLY WINS THE PRESIDENCY

On March 26, 2000, the third direct presidential election in Russia's brief democratic history took place. Voters went to 90,000 polling stations spread across 11 time zones. Of the 108 million eligible voters, 68 percent turned out, well above the 50 percent required for the ballot to be valid. When 70 percent of the vote had been counted, Putin had won 51.7 percent, just over the 50 percent he needed to avoid a runoff on April 16. In second place, with 30 percent, was the Communist leader Gennady Zyuganov, who complained of widespread fraud. The Moscow liberal, Grigory Yavlinsky, trailed far behind in third place, with 5.78 percent of the vote. According to the *Manchester Guardian* newspaper, Putin supporters had feared that Yavlinsky might win enough votes to force a runoff. In the final days of the campaign, state-run television smeared Yavlinsky, claiming he was supported by homosexuals and Jews and funded by foreigners.

Acting president Vladimir Putin shakes hands with Siberian oil workers during his 2000 campaign.

Within weeks of Putin's election, even before his inauguration, Putin made his first visit to the West, traveling to London, England. He told reporters from National Public Radio news that Europe would pay for ignoring the cause of Russia's war in Chechnya, "Islamic terrorism," a term rarely heard before the September 11, 2001, attack on the World Trade Center in

New York City. During Putin's visit, members of Great Britain's Muslim community protested his appearances, chanting "jihad [holy war] for Russia." Putin fired back at a press conference, saying, "The actions of Russia in the Chechen republic is the return of civilization to that place."

On May 7, Putin formally assumed the presidency. In a gilded Kremlin chamber once used to crown tsars, with his hand placed on Russia's constitution, Putin took a presidential oath that said in part: "I swear to safeguard human rights, defend Russia's independence and faithfully serve the people." Mindful that many still suspected he was Yeltsin's lackey, National Public Radio news reported that Putin emphasized in his inaugural speech the constitutionality of his victory. "Today is really an historical day," he said. "For the first time in the history of our state, power is being transferred in the most democratic and simple way, by people's will, lawfully and peacefully. We have proven that Russia is a real modern, democratic state." At age 47, Vladimir V. Putin was president of Russia.

"He projected the image of a young, healthy, very ordinary man from the KGB—which for the majority of the electorate would mean that he would not be corrupted—and a man who hates Chechens and adores the Russian army. It was a primitive but effective PR campaign," said Moscow journalist Nataliya Gevorkyan.

Russian politician Igor Artemyev put an even simpler spin on the meaning of the election. He said Russians had elected Putin with a sense of relief. After Yeltsin, Artemyev said to National Public Radio news, "the country demanded a more austere leader, and that's what we got. After the flamboyant Siberian bear, the totally unpredictable Yeltsin who would drink a lot, get up and conduct an orchestra and then land in the hospital, we got another type. We got a strict ruler who doesn't smile."

# CHAPTER

# 8

# The Sinking of the *Kursk*

ON THE MORNING OF AUGUST 10, 2000, THE RUSSIAN CRUISE-MISSILE submarine *Kursk*, under the command of Captain Gennadiy P. Liachin, left its base for practice exercises in the Barents Sea, an arm of the Arctic Ocean, north of Norway and European Russia. On board were 118 men—111 crew members, 5 officers, and 2 engineers.

Liachin expected a good run. Just a few weeks before, his men had been recognized as the best submarine crew of the Northern Fleet. "I want to serve on a submarine until retirement," senior petty officer Rishat Zubaydullin wrote to his mother shortly before the submarine left port. Seaman Roman Martynov joined the *Kursk* straight from a stay in a hospital. BBC News reported that he wrote to his mother: "We will spend three days at sea, but don't worry mum." At an unhurried pace, the submarine proceeded to a location northeast of the seaport city of Murmansk.

To World War II merchant seamen, Murmansk was a name associated with disaster. Forty Allied convoys, with a total of more than 800 ships, including 350 under the U.S. flag, were scheduled for a Murmansk run from 1941 through 1945. Their mission was to reach Murmansk and supply the Russian army as it battled Germans on the eastern front. The route through the Barents Sea proved deadly. German fighter and bomber planes, stationed on the coast of Norway, pounded the ships as they rounded the coast. Aided by constant daylight, the attackers were often able to refuel three times during a single assault. Mariners whose ships were badly hit were often forced to leap into blazing oil slicks, or else into freezing open water, the temperature of which caused death in minutes. By war's end, 97 ships lay at the bottom of the Barents Sea, sunk by bombs, torpedoes, mines, and the fury of wind and water.

On the night of Saturday, August 12, 2000, the *Kursk* radioed its position from 100 miles out to sea: 69°40' N, 37°35' E. By coincidence, the location was not far from where the British sloop *Lark* had sunk the German submarine *U-425* with 53 men aboard in February 1945. The *Kursk* requested permission to begin a practice night attack on surface ships 30 miles away, led by the heavy nuclear-missile cruiser *Petr Velikiy*. "Dobro," came the reply, meaning "good."

Two thousand miles to the south, Vladimir Putin was vacationing near the Black Sea, a favorite resort area for Russians. The weather was hot and sunny, and the usually pale, five-foot, six-inch-tall Putin was tanning on the beach.

## PUTIN'S EARLY ACTS AS PRESIDENT

In the months since his election, Putin had continued his course of centralizing power within the federal government. In his usual steady style, he did little to make critics think that he was an antidemocratic authoritarian. On the other hand, a pattern of cinching tight the saddle of his administration gave rise to concerns.

U.S. President Bill Clinton and Vladimir Putin take part in a signing ceremony in the Kremlin on June 4, 2000. The leaders signed agreements to dispose of 68 tons of weapons-grade plutonium and share early-warning data on missile and space launches.

Within days after his inauguration, for example, Putin sent agents to search the offices of Russia's biggest independent media group, allegedly as part of some vague criminal investigation. Eventually, he succeeded in shutting down Vladimir Gusinsky's media conglomerate, Media-Most. Weeks later, the tax police searched the offices of environmental organizations, and the Kremlin abolished two environmental oversight bodies in the name of bureaucratic streamlining. By summer, the Duma had given him broad powers to fire regional governors, whom Putin had long accused of putting personal and provincial interests ahead of the good of the whole country.

While he worked to maintain his political standing at home, Putin also sought to strengthen his country's hand abroad, especially with the West. In June 2000, he hosted U.S. president Bill Clinton for a three-day summit, during which Clinton took Russians' questions on a call-in news show. Although the two leaders signed a pair of arms control agreements, they remained far apart on the summit's central issue: America's interest in building a national missile defense system.

The military was a problem for Putin. Winning the war in Chechnya—one of the few campaign promises he had allowed himself to make—demanded a well-trained, well-equipped army, something the Russian economy could not afford. The United States' talk of building a massive missile defense system—"Star Wars," as it was nicknamed—had been the straw that broke the back of the Soviet Union. Putin was not going to let himself be intimidated by the issue, but at the same time, his administration could not afford an arms race while it also tried to upgrade its forces and convert to a market economy.

The Russian military was in miserable condition. Military spending had plummeted by about 75 percent since Soviet-era days to around $4 billion, less than 3 percent of Russia's gross domestic product. Soldiers took second jobs to earn extra money. Junior officers resigned, creating a gap in expertise. In Chechnya, spare parts were so hard to find that soldiers often took them from wrecked vehicles.

## NEWS OF THE *KURSK* ARRIVES

On Saturday, August 12, 2000, around midnight, as Putin continued his vacation, trying to set aside the cares of his office for a while, the Norwegian Seismic Array (NORSCAR) recorded an explosion of 1.5 on the Richter scale. Two minutes later, a second shock of about the same magnitude occurred. Near the *Kursk*'s location, three submarines on spy duty—USS *Memphis*, USS *Toledo*, and HMS *Splendid*—reported that they had detected underwater blasts. The American submarines speculated that the sounds were a submarine's ballast tanks blowing apart, followed by the revving of the propeller.

On board the *Kursk*, there was pandemonium. The combat alarm sounded when explosions tore a gash in the outer shell of the submarine from the front section all the way to the conning tower, killing about 40 men. Other crew members ran toward the stern, slamming the compartment doors shut behind them. As seawater poured into five of the submarine's nine compartments, the nose of the 14,000-ton *Kursk* dipped toward the ocean floor 400 feet below.

Twenty-three men stumbled into a secure compartment near the stern. One found a pencil and paper and described over several hours the worsening condition of the survivors. In the darkness, his handwriting strayed all over the paper. When the oxygen was almost gone, he put his notes in a plastic bag and sealed it. The *Kursk* rolled over 25 degrees on its port side and rested in the ooze at the bottom of the Barents Sea.

By the evening of August 14, the sinking of the *Kursk* was world news. Canada, France, Germany, Great Britain, Israel, Italy, the Netherlands, Norway, Sweden, the United States, and other countries offered their assistance. On news programs in the United States, naval experts voiced cautious opinions that if the submarine could be reached in time, the men aboard might be saved. One report from the Russian Northern Fleet announced that tapping sounds had been heard on the hull. The Russians responded that they had the situation well in hand. The world was talking constantly about the incident, but from Putin, the silence was deafening.

He later said that he wanted to go to the site immediately, but his advisors convinced him not to cut short his vacation. They recommended that he meet with the families of the victims instead. The days went by, and Putin continued his stay by the Black Sea, leaving it to the Russian government to issue statements and respond to offers of assistance from foreign countries.

## THE WORLD RESPONDS TO THE TRAGEDY

"The whole country is on edge over this thing. It's terrible—imagine dying that way?" a security guard in Moscow told CNN.

"My heart is aching for those 118 people on board," said a World War II veteran who had served in the Soviet navy. "I turn on the television a hundred times a day, I just don't know what can be done. I don't have words to express what I feel."

By Wednesday, August 16, Russian naval officials knew the truth—the crew was dead—but they seemed to be paralyzed and unable to admit it. Putin returned to Moscow. On Friday, a spokesperson for the Russian Northern Fleet held a press conference that lasted just four minutes. A deputy prime minister tried to meet with distraught families and was heckled. One woman fainted, with tears streaming down her face. When the weekend newspapers hit the streets in Russia, editorial writers expressed outrage. "The reflexes of the Russian elite have not changed in the last 10 or 15 years. . . . The first thing they want to do is to conceal the truth," the leading daily newspaper *Izvestiya* said on its front page. Pointing out that Putin had not called the situation "critical" until Wednesday, the British Broadcasting Corporation (BBC) reported, "Then the Russian and world press rose up to ask: 'Why does the Russian president allow himself to ignore the tragedy so blatantly?'"

## PUTIN RESPONDS AT LAST

On the following Tuesday, when Putin finally traveled to the scene of the "rescue" efforts, which, by now, were ship salvage efforts, the BBC ran the jeering headline, "Putin Struggles to Express Emotion."

> This was his chance to show the emotion that the Russian public has been waiting to see from its leader, and he dressed in black for the first time. His only earlier effort to capture the national mood of impending tragedy—more than a week after the submarine sank—was woefully inadequate. 'We are all following the tragedy now unfolding in the Barents Sea with aching hearts, and without any exaggeration, with tears in our eyes,' he said on Sunday. But there were no tears in Mr.

Putin meets with relatives of dead seamen from the *Kursk* on August 22, 2000. The nuclear submarine exploded during torpedo firing exercises, registering 4.4 on the Richter scale, and sinking to a depth of 108 meters.

Putin's eyes, and nothing to erase the image of the tanned president in his shirtsleeves, relaxing on the Black Sea coast in the first days after the *Kursk* crisis broke. Instead, his failure to become engaged—and in particular his failure to return to Moscow until last Wednesday, four days after the *Kursk* sank—has been widely interpreted as callous indifference."

Too late, Putin tried to reassure the Russian public that everything possible had been done, though for once, his characteristically blunt style did not play well. He said there had been little hope for the 118 crew members from the start, and that he had asked Defense Minister Igor Sergeyev about chances for saving the *Kursk* and the crew the moment he was informed about the disaster. According to CNN.com, Putin said: "The answer was, 'There is an extremely small chance for rescue but it exists.'" He repeated that his wish was to fly to the scene, but he chose not to go, on the advice of others. He added that placing blame would not do any good now.

Still, there was no denying that the sinking of the *Kursk* had been Putin's first major domestic crisis and he had bungled it, not just politically, but personally. Ironically, his seriousness, which voters had seen as a welcome change, compared with Boris Yeltsin's reputation for partying, worked against Putin when the public wanted compassion.

Three weeks later, he flew to the United States on a pre-scheduled visit. Appearing on the *Larry King Live* show on September 8, he addressed King's questions about the *Kursk*. Putin said that if he had it to do over again, he might have acted differently—and certainly would have ended his vacation earlier. "But again, this would have been a PR [public relations] action," CNN.com quoted him as saying, "since in any city of the country or throughout the world, I'm always linked to the military. . . . From the point of view of PR, that could look better. Maybe yes it would look better."

He was not alone in his convictions, especially among higher-ups in the Russian military. The following day, the Russian newspaper *Krasnaya Zvezda* asked Colonel General Valery Manilov, senior deputy chief of the general staff, "Who is going to shoulder responsibility for the tragedy?" Manilov answered that the country's leadership and the armed forces already had.

"The president has done something without analogues in the latest history," he said. "Instead of turning up at the site of the tragedy as modern PR rules dictate—it earned him criticism from moralists in the West—he went directly to the perished submariners' widows, parents, and relatives. He was with them and talked to them that horrible night when it became apparent that nobody in the *Kursk* had survived.

"This is what I call true responsibility," said the general.

# 9

# Pivotal Moments in Putin's Presidency

**THROUGHOUT 2002, PUTIN MANAGED TO MAKE A PRO-WESTERN SHIFT IN** foreign affairs, but he still had difficulty defining his stance at home. He couldn't shake his Russian patriot roots, even though he longed to advocate for Western things. It was difficult to break the old ways, like bartering with special-interest groups.

One of Putin's most notable achievements of 2002 was the ban placed on capital punishment. He also allowed the Russian people to open bank accounts abroad. But at home he implemented housing reforms and raised the rent of some of the residents of the city of Voronezh. During the spring, they took to the streets in protest, the first public protest of his presidency. Controls were placed on the governors of the various regions, limiting their powers and forcing them to report to overseers Putin had appointed.

"In what President Bush said and what I said, there is something in common, which is the following: We all recognize that terrorism has taken on an international character."

—Vladimir Putin

At the time, some expressed fears that Russia was turning into a police state. They cited the closing of the last national TV station, TV-6, ending free media expression. Other organizations that opposed the Kremlin's policies were also shut down. A group of businessmen, powerful during Yeltsin's administration, joined to buy a new, private TV station. Putin approved this station grudgingly, but he made sure that two men who agreed with his policies sat on the board of directors, ensuring censorship.

He was running what some journalists felt was a neutralizing government, a blend of old and new that was his way of maintaining calm in the country. Lilia Shevtsova wrote in 2003, "His hybrid political regime . . . linked conservatives and modernizers. It was an instrument to neutralize conflicts." This tendency to try to please all of the people all of the time had journalists labeling him "the two-headed eagle" and referring to him as having "skis that go in different directions."

One of the directions led directly to the United States and his warm rapport with President George W. Bush. He referred to their joint worldview: that terrorism is the biggest threat to international security. In an interview with the *Wall Street Journal* on February 11, 2002, he said, "In what President Bush said and what I said, there is something in common, which is the following: We all recognize that terrorism has taken on an international character." At the time, Putin reminded reporters that he had spoken of the "arc of instability" in the world, similar to Bush's comment about an "axis of evil." Despite his endorsement of Bush's actions, he seemed to disapprove of the Bush administration's approach, and of the fact that Bush's "axis" included former Russian allies.

Some believed that Putin was simply sending a subtle message that he would support the United States, especially if Russian financial interests were taken care of. Although they came from completely different backgrounds, these two leaders unexpectedly found themselves on common ground, with similar goals.

Perhaps it was because of this cooperation that the Bush administration never did diminish the security and economic assistance programs established by former President Bill Clinton, as Bush had threatened the year before. Bush also encouraged private investment in Russian companies and asked Congress to dismiss the Jackson-Vanik Amendment (which tied trade to Jewish emigration numbers). These requests encouraged normal trade relations between the two countries.

Even as the White House continued to praise and support Russia, voices within the Russian government complained that Putin was giving in too easily to U.S. demands. For example, Russia now supported military bases in central Asia and the Republic of Georgia, the enlargement of NATO (the North Atlantic Treaty Organization), and the repeal of the Anti-Ballistic Missile Treaty. Putin was giving a lot, while getting little, according to some of his countrymen.

In the West, critics also felt the relationship was one-sided, but they felt more strongly about the fact that it was based solely on antiterrorism measures. They thought there was nothing more substantial going on. The past distrust continued to raise its head in relationships between Moscow and Washington.

In May of 2002, Putin and Bush met in Moscow to discuss nuclear nonproliferation. They ultimately signed the Strategic

Offensive Reduction Treaty, agreeing to reduce their arsenals to between 1,700 and 2,200 warheads each by December 2012. Called the Treaty of Moscow, it was written using the honor system. In other words, there was no way for either country to ensure that the other was complying with the document. At this summit, they also signed a declaration promising to work together on security issues and set a basis for dealing jointly with new issues. Nothing was done at this time to eradicate the Jackson-Vanik Amendment, which Putin had sorely hoped would happen. He said to reporters on May 26, "We are not thrilled that this did not happen."

Shortly after the summit, Putin realized one of his biggest dreams. The European Union (EU) recognized Russia's market-economy status and Bush personally called Putin in June to tell him that Washington had done the same thing. This recognition would give Russian companies wider access in the West. It could mean more than $1.5 billion each year in increased revenue. It also could mean that Russia might be eligible to join the World Trade Organization (WTO), one of Putin's goals. Conditions for membership in the WTO included the provision that Russian markets be opened, which could be difficult for Russians unused to competition in the marketplace.

That spring, Russia participated in its first NATO summit. Putin's remarks were positive and supportive, even though he followed his statement by stressing that Russia's cooperation didn't automatically mean unconditional support for every NATO action. He said, "We've come a long way from confrontation to dialogue and from confrontation to cooperation."

The Group of Eight (G-8) meeting was held that year in June in Canada. Russia had been admitted to the group in recognition of Putin's pro-Western stance. He was promised at the meeting $20 billion to "safeguard and dismantle Russian weapons of mass destruction, linked to the fulfillment of its nonproliferation obligations." Russia hosted the 2006 summit in St. Petersburg on July 15-17.

Russian President Vladimir Putin and U.S. President George W. Bush exchange a friendly handshake in June 2001. The international war on terrorism launched as a result of the September 11, 2001, terrorist attacks on the United States brought the two men closer.

Throughout all of these major world events, many still questioned Putin's philosophies and their staying power. The *Economist* wrote on May 16, 2002: "Relations between Russia and the West have rarely been better. But what does it mean in practice? And can it last? . . . The real danger is not that Russia's march to the West goes into reverse, but that it bogs down for lack of ideas and people." It is believed that the Kremlin doesn't trust the Russian people to understand the reasoning behind policy changes, so it doesn't bother to explain anything to them. Or else, the government simply doesn't trust its people.

At home, Putin was faced with Boris Yeltsin's return to the public eye. Yeltsin had lost weight and seemed healthier. He also seemed to promote Prime Minister Mikhail Kasyanov as a candidate to replace Putin. Putin met the implicit challenge with his usual stoic demeanor, saying at his June 24 press conference, "Yeltsin is a free individual who can move about, meet with anyone, and express his opinion. We respect his opinion. However, I have my own opinion, and I will do what I think is best for Russia now and in the future."

Throughout the fall of 2002, Putin resumed trade negotiations with Iraq and announced that he would expand nuclear assistance to Iran. He also announced plans to link Russia's railroad system with rail lines in North Korea, prompting *Newsweek* to write that Russia was creating its "own axis of friendship."

By the end of 2002, Russia and the United States were at odds over the United States' plans to take military action in Iraq. Putin agreed to stop trying to save Saddam Hussein's regime only after the United States guaranteed it would not interfere with Russian economic interests.

Throughout his administration, Putin has walked a tightrope between pleasing his friends in the West as well as the Russian people at home. Putin has had to deal with protests and complaints about low salaries, corruption within the justice system and among the police, lack of heat and electricity in some areas, and lack of funding for education, defense, and scientific research. Pensioners, those Russian citizens receiving social services and financial help from the government, also have protested the cuts in their benefits, including housing and prescription subsidies and access to free public transportation. Many in the military are also angry over cuts in their benefits.

Putin often responds to criticisms by pointing out Western shortcomings. For example, he has compared the elections in the Ukraine with the disputed 2000 U.S. presidential election.

He lost some of the people's approval when his government seized the oil company Yukos and arrested Mikhail Khodorkovsky, the company's principal owner. One of the prime reasons Khodorkovsky was arrested was to make an example for other Russian businessmen who became too embroiled in politics. It worked.

Late in 2004, the Ukrainian presidential election was held. During the campaigns by democratic candidate Viktor Yushchenko and Prime Minister Viktor Yanukovich, most opinion polls showed a significant lead for Yushchenko, if there was a fair and honest election. Putin strongly campaigned for Yanukovich and compelled Russian businesses to donate about $300 million for that campaign. As the campaign wore on, Yushchenko's appearance changed drastically. His formerly handsome face became pockmarked and bloated. It was discovered that he was suffering from dioxin poisoning, assumed to be an opposition plot to kill him. Yanukovich won the election, but the result was annulled because of fraud during the campaign. Yushchenko won by a wide margin in the second vote, taken several days later. Putin's aggressive campaigning in a fraudulent campaign cost him approval ratings at home.

## THE TRAGEDY AT BESLAN

It was the first day of school in Beslan, a town of about 30,000 in the region of Ossetia, about 30 miles east of Chechnya. Early in the morning of September 1, 2004, as parents brought their children to the brick, two-story School Number One, more than two dozen Chechen gunmen herded hundreds of the students, their parents, and teachers into the gym.

By this point in the ongoing conflict over Chechnya's independence, Russians in the region had become used to the bloodshed, fighting, and attacks against civilians. Just the day before the siege began, Putin had given a speech in which he said, "We shall fight them (Chechen terrorists), throw them in prison and destroy them." There were possible links to Al Qaeda, and Chechen terrorists had grown ever more bold in their attacks and suicide bombings. But on that first day of September, an event was about to unfold that shocked even battle-hardened Russians.

About 1,200 hostages were crowded into the gym. As the word got out about the attack, Russian officials went on television and lied to the people, deliberately lowering the number of hostages in an attempt to maintain calm. The terrorists were watching, however, and were angry over the lies that only a small number of people were being held. They assumed that meant that the military was intending to attack the building.

President Putin waited 24 hours before addressing the situation publicly. When he finally appeared on TV, he said, "Our principal task in the current situation is of course to save the lives and health of the hostages." Officials at this time were debating whether or not to let the terrorists go, giving them a plane, money, and releasing 30 of their colleagues from jail. But others argued for negotiations. Since it wasn't really clear what the terrorists wanted, there was no way to know just how to begin.

The situation in the gym was uncomfortable, dangerous, and very tense. Children were starting to suffer from lack of food and water. The temperature climbed, and the hostages began to peel off layers of clothing in the stuffy space. The school's principal, Lydia Tsaliyeva, remained calm and tried begging for the children, asking the guerillas to allow the

Putin believed that the Beslan hostage crisis was a result of a weak country. Many believe his statements following the tragedy set back the democratic process in Russia.

children to go free. "Feel mercy for the young," she begged. One of the leaders reportedly answered her, "Who felt mercy for my children? My house was bombed and five of my children were killed."

Some Russian officials decided to "fight fire with fire" and gathered together the terrorists' wives and children and told them their families would be killed if the hostages were not released. Even though they televised the threat, and the terrorists could see their loved ones being threatened, the ruse didn't work because the rebels didn't seem to care if their wives and children were killed or not.

Nearly two days after the siege began, Putin called in Ruslan Aushev, a war hero and former resident of the region of Ingushetia, who had previously been on good terms with Chechnya. When Aushev arrived in Beslan, he was admitted to the school to talk to one of the spokesmen for the terrorists. Aushev noted the deteriorating condition in the gym, saying later that the children had stripped down to their underwear by this time because of the heat in the gym, and they were being forced to drink their own urine because they still had not been given any water.

Aushev was given a demand letter written by the Chechen rebel leader, Shamil Basayev. According to some, he was the equivalent of Osama bin Laden, directly responsible for suicide bombings and other attacks on Russian civilians that had left hundreds dead. Basayev demanded withdrawal of Russian troops from Chechnya, which would then be granted its independence. The letter claimed that hostages would only be released once Putin had declared that troops would be pulled out of the region.

When Aushev left, he was allowed to take 25 of the youngest children with him. He also took some of the mothers who had brought babies with them.

On the third night, two bombs were exploded within the gym, killing dozens of hostages instantly. Parts of the roof fell in and some children tried to escape through the windows. Some of them were shot. Outside the school, Russian soldiers and civilians who had armed themselves and gathered there to wait held back at first, unsure of what was happening. But then

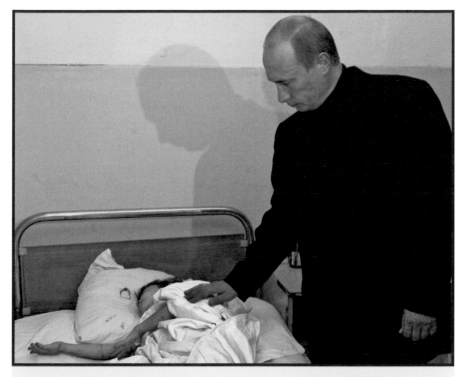

A victim of the Beslan hostage crisis receives a hospital visit from President Putin on September 4, 2004.

they tried to protect some of the escaping children. Both sides believed the other had started an attack, and initially, each side tried to keep the situation from getting any worse.

But it was too late. Some of the soldiers later said how difficult it was to kill the terrorists without harming the hostages. There were so many, and it was dark and chaotic. Finally, the roof of the gym caved in completely. Cars drove up to the school and tried to evacuate as many hostages as they could, as the battle continued to rage around them.

In the end, 30 of the 32 terrorists were killed. One of the two survivors was killed by angry civilians as he was being led from the scene. The only survivor was a 24-year-old former Russian soldier who had lived in Chechnya. In all, 338 innocent civilians were killed, most of them children.

Putin never again appeared publicly during the siege to reassure the country or explain what was happening. Once the battle was over, he flew to the hospital where survivors were being treated.

More than a day after the siege ended, he addressed the nation, calling the attack "unprecedented in its inhumanity and cruelty." He said, "We need to admit that we did not fully understand the complexity and the dangers of the processes at work in our own country and in the world . . . we were unable to react adequately. We showed ourselves to be weak. And the weak get beaten." He blamed this weakness on the collapse of the Soviet Union and the many transitions taking place in the country including within its economics and politics. More than a week later, he announced a plan for fighting terrorism in Russia: He would put tighter controls on government, including eliminating direct elections of governing individuals. He claimed it would promote unity and create "a single chain of command." Many believe it was actually a step backward for the democratic process in Russia.

# 10

# Putin and the New Russia

**SEARCHING FOR PERSONAL CLUES TO VLADIMIR PUTIN CAN BE FRUSTRATING.**
All that he does seems to be rooted in one devotion: his love for
Russia. Those who know Putin well tend to offer little more than
what was heard about him during his days as a bureaucrat in St.
Petersburg. He is admired and praised, and appears to believe
in hard work and self-sacrificing loyalty. Even foreigners use
similar words to describe him. "I found him great to deal with,
compared with these other Russian bureaucrats who all wanted
to fleece you," said Graham Humes, an American who set up
a charity in St. Petersburg, in the *New York Times Magazine*.
"He was very intense; he controls everything in the room. You
felt he wanted to be feared but didn't want to give you cause
to fear him."

Concerning his future as president of Russia and as a world
leader, his old mentor, former St. Petersburg mayor Anatoly
Sobchak, offered an insight into Putin that makes him a little

Vladimir Putin is flanked by Ukrainian Prime Minister Viktor Yanukovich (left) and Ukrainian President Leonid Kuchma as they walk in the Ukrainian port of Kerch, Crimea, on November 12, 2004.

more understandable, to Americans at least. According to the *New York Times Magazine*, Sobchak predicted, "He will govern both as Teddy Roosevelt and as FDR." What he meant, Sobchak said, is that Putin will be as concerned as Theodore Roosevelt was with strengthening the state and taking on the "malefactors of great wealth." Like Franklin Roosevelt, on the other hand, he will try to use the state's power to rebuild a country that has fallen from great economic heights to poverty and mass unemployment.

Many believe that Putin does not yearn for a return to the days of the USSR. CNN.com said that he has stated that "anyone who doesn't regret the passing of the Soviet Union has no heart, but that anyone who wants it restored has no brains."

Yet it is not as plain as what he learned from witnessing the last days of the Soviet Union, either. He saw how the planned economies of the Eastern bloc countries, in which the state dictated all matters of production and price, gradually fell into disrepair. In St. Petersburg, he was part of Russia's rocky transition to a free-market, democratic system, and he saw how easily greed can overtake idealism.

In his first state of the nation address, Putin painted a bleak picture of the country that included falling standards of living and plummeting life expectancy and birth rates. He conceded that "there is no alternative" to free-market democracy, especially in light of Russia's ailing economy, but he has also argued the need to rebuild the role of a strong state. "Only a strong government—and if you don't like the word strong, let's say effective government—can protect people's political and economic freedoms," he said in the *Washington Post*. A strong state is a Russian tradition, he maintains, and is needed because the Russian economy has become "criminalized" by corruption. He will not revert to totalitarianism to root out corruption, though. "He's too sophisticated, he's too modern, he's too Western oriented, he's too young to be any kind of old-style Soviet dictator," remarked Carnegie Foundation analyst Michael McFaul on National Public Radio news. "But what worries me is what happens when democracy becomes inconvenient for what he wants to do in other agenda areas?"

In fact, Putin expresses less enthusiasm for democracy than he does for order. Several times, he has warned against partisanship—a natural force in democracy—and insisted that "civil accord" must not be disturbed.

## RUSSIA'S RELATIONSHIP WITH THE WEST

To help keep Russia on an even keel domestically and economically, Putin knows that a solid relationship with the United States is key. His aims—ending the decline of Russian power, while also avoiding another superpower competition with the

United States—both contribute to a good relationship. On a practical level, he avoids criticism of the West because Russia is not in a position to make enemies.

Still, Putin harbors a centuries-old Russian mistrust of the motives of foreigners—the United States, in particular. "There is now a firm consensus view at the highest level that Russia must make its own economic and security decisions," said Swedish-born investor Peter Castenfeld in the *New York Times Magazine*. Castenfeld has worked closely with successive Russian governments, including Putin's.

> At the root of this view lies the perception that the West, in particular America, misused its position of power under labels like "strategic partnership" and "free market reform" when Russia was weak. . . . This isn't seen by them as being anti-American. They just think America is so powerful that it is unpredictable, because it is able to project domestic political needs into the international arena at will. So they want to strengthen the state—to make the economy work better, be more rule-based and market-oriented. They also want to strongly resist increased geostrategic pressure on their neighbors.

As a rule, Putin makes an effort to avoid strained relations with the United States. In December 2000, he granted a pardon to American Edmond Pope, who spent eight months in prison on a 20-year sentence for espionage. In March 2001, when former FBI agent Robert Hanssen was charged with espionage, the United States and Russia each expelled the other's diplomats, but Putin pointedly said that he did not think the episode would damage the nations' relationship.

Some believe that Putin's address to the Federation Assembly on April 3, 2001, signified a turning point in his presidency. He was no longer stiff and reserved. He was dynamic and is remembered for his advocacy of the market and his support of the renewal of economic reforms stalled in the previous

Presidents Putin and Bush exchange arms treaties at the Kremlin on May 24, 2002. The treaties decreased the number of strategic nuclear warheads over 10 years by one-third.

administration. He promised to put an end to the habit of bureaucrats taking bribes in exchange for lobbying to reform the government. He also presented a package of new laws that covered reform of the judicial system, pension and tax reforms, and regulation of business and labor and industry.

By June 2001, when Putin hosted President Bush at the first United States-Russia summit of the twenty-first century, the focus was squarely on alliance. A month later, when the two leaders met again, they still had their differences, however. Even so, both men emphasized their nations' growing economic ties and agreed that talks about a missile defense system should be paired with talks aimed at reducing nuclear stockpiles.

"More than a decade after the Cold War ended, it is time to move beyond suspicion and toward straight talk; beyond mutually assured destruction and toward mutually earned respect," Bush contended. According to National Public Radio (NPR) news, Putin responded, "Russia and the United States are not enemies. They do not threaten each other. And they could be fully good allies."

## THE FIGHT AGAINST TERRORISM

More than anything, what has brought the United States and Russia closer together were the attacks on the World Trade Center and the Pentagon on September 11, 2001.

According to Lawrence Sheets of NPR, "Putin's support for the U.S.-led antiterrorist alliance has brought Russia and the West closer than at any time since World War II." The attacks "had a profound effect on both presidents," said NPR's Mike Shuster. "They convinced President Putin of the reality of new international threats. They convinced President Bush to move away from unilateralism in international affairs to work closely with many nations, especially Russia."

After the September 11 attacks, Putin and Bush saw eye to eye on how the United States should respond. Putin has long branded Chechen fighters as terrorists linked to Islamic fundamentalists— among them, Osama bin Laden, who was behind the September 11 attacks. Putin was instrumental in giving the United States a free hand in pursuing the terrorists in Afghanistan, even though the conflict took place near Russia's border. When Putin sees the United States battling bin Laden, said defense analyst Alexander Goltz to NPR, Putin is quick "to say, 'We are fighting the same war, we are fighting the same people, we are fighting international terrorist conspiracy. We were the first victim, you are the second.'"

## THE FUTURE FOR RUSSIA—AND PUTIN

In Russia, Putin seems to be receiving generally high marks. Moscow journalist Nataliya Gevorkyan, who cowrote Putin's campaign biography, said that Russians realize that Putin will make some mistakes. "How can a KGB vice-colonel be prepared to become president of a huge and problematic country?" she told NPR. "There's no way. And short periods as the director of the FSB [which succeeded the KGB], and as prime minister, do not help. These were just the formal, necessary steps for those who moved him to power, because the man could not appear from nowhere. Really, his public service career had consisted of being one of the bureaucrats who worked for St. Petersburg's first democratic mayor, Anatoly Sobchak; you hardly can compare this responsibility with the responsibility of the president of the country. For an amateur, I think he has managed rather successfully to grow into a new role—and he really enjoys it."

Moreover, human-rights activist Sergei Kovalev believes that Russians are not as eager to embrace Western-style democracy as Americans would like them to be. In an article in the *New York Review of Books*, Kovalev summed up Russian attitudes: "We don't want to return to communism, but we're fed up with your democracy, your freedom, your human rights. What we want is order."

When Putin appeared on the *Larry King Live* show in September 2000, King asked him a question that would have been unthinkable only 15 years ago when the official stance of the Soviet Union on religion was atheism.

King asked, "Do you believe in a higher power?" Putin replied, "I believe in human beings. I believe in His good intentions. I believe in the fact that all of us have come to this world to do good. And if we do so, and if we do so together, then success is waiting for us. . . . And most important; we will achieve the ultimate goal—comfort in our own heart."

The man who made a meteoric rise from unknown spy to president of Russia was initially embraced by the people simply because he was the complete opposite of Boris Yeltsin, the president everyone had tired of because of his boorish ways.

President Vladimir Putin walks through St. George's Hall in the Kremlin to take part in the inauguration ceremony for his second term on May 7, 2004.

They felt that in Putin they were getting the relative calm and stability they longed for.

While President Putin was able to establish some of that calm, he also damaged his presidency by his withdrawn nature and inability to relate warmly with his people.

Although the Russian constitution limits the president to two four-year terms, just like in the United States, it is widely speculated that Putin won't abide by that law but may find a way to remain in office and in power. He denies that he will do this, but as his past performance shows, he sometimes acts in unexpected ways.

The author Lilia Shevtsova calls Putin's style of government "imitation democracy." While the government operates on democratic principles, it does so without what she calls its "inconveniences." Russian television contains fancy graphics but uses scripts dictated by Kremlin overseers. Elections have multiple candidates, but the outcomes are often rigged. The legal system uses judges and juries, but corruption is widespread.

Putin stresses the need for stability, yet terror attacks have increased during his tenure, causing many to question whether the country can be stable if it is not safe. By late 2004, some in his administration admitted that Russia wasn't ready for the democratic "experiment." They claimed that Putin's popularity was based on the fact that the Russian people were happy to let this calm man do more or less what he wanted as long as their lives weren't disrupted too much or too often.

It is still difficult to figure out just who Vladimir Putin is as a leader. In his restrictions against the media and decision to do away with regional elections, he seems more like a controlling Communist leader. He is very authoritarian and stubborn, and he can be almost paranoid in his beliefs that all criticisms are made by political enemies. Yet, in some of his other moves, such as his close dealings with the West and cutting some of the benefits put into place by the Communists, he seems more progressive.

When Boris Yeltsin named Putin his chosen successor, he said, "He will be able to unite around himself those who will revive Great Russia in the new twenty-first century." Only time will tell whether Yeltsin was right, and whether Putin was indeed the right man at the right time, whether he was the right president to lead the Russian people from their oppressed past and into the new century and a new, democratic way of life.

# CHRONOLOGY

| | |
|---|---|
| **1952** | Born October 7 in Leningrad (now St. Petersburg), the child of a factory foreman and his wife. |
| **1975** | Graduates from the law department of Leningrad State University; joins the KGB's Foreign Intelligence Service. |
| **1983** | Marries Lyudmila, a specialist in foreign languages. |
| **1985–1990** | Assigned to work for the KGB in East Germany. |
| **1990** | Becomes assistant rector for international affairs at Leningrad State University. He also serves as an adviser to the chairman of the Leningrad City Council. |
| **1991–1994** | Serves as chairman of the Foreign Relations Committee of the St. Petersburg mayor's office. |
| **1991** | Resigns from the KGB August 20. |
| **1994–1996** | Serves as first deputy chairman of the St. Petersburg city government and chairman of the Committee for External Relations. |
| **1996** | Transfers to Moscow in August to work as President Boris Yeltsin's first deputy manager. |
| **1997** | Becomes Yeltsin's deputy chief of staff in charge of the Main Control Department in March. |
| **1998** | Named presidential first deputy chief of staff in charge of Russian regions in May. |
| **1998–1999** | Serves as director of the Federal Security Service, a successor agency to the KGB. |
| **1999** | *March–August.* Serves as Russian Security Council secretary. |
| | *August.* Appointed prime minister. |
| | *December 31.* Named acting president, pending elections, by Yeltsin, who abruptly resigns. |
| **2000** | *March 26.* Elected president of Russia. Wins in the first round, capturing just over 50 percent of the vote. |

**2000**   *April.* Defends war in Chechnya during a visit to London, his first trip to the West since being elected.

*May 7.* Sworn in as Russia's second democratically elected president.

*June.* Holds a summit in Moscow with U.S. president Bill Clinton. The leaders sign two arms control agreements but disagree on U.S. plans for a national missile defense system.

*July 18.* Putin and Chinese president Jiang Zemin sign a joint statement opposing U.S. plans to build missile shields over North America and Asia.

*August 12.* The Russian submarine *Kursk* sinks in the Barents Sea, with a crew of 118 aboard. Putin says he feels responsible but denies taking too long with rescue efforts.

*December.* Meets in Cuba with Fidel Castro, reestablishing ties between Havana and Moscow that broke down when the Soviet Union collapsed.

**2001**   *March.* The United States and Russia expel 50 of each other's diplomats over alleged espionage. Putin downplays the expulsions' effects on ties between the nations.

*March 28.* Announces the biggest cabinet shake-up since his election. Among the changes, he appoints Russia's first civilian defense minister.

*April.* Accused of silencing the press when the Russian government takes over the NTV television station and cracks down on other independent media outlets.

*June 16.* Says Russia and the United States "are not enemies" during his first summit with U.S. President George W. Bush.

2001    *September.* Pledges to help the U.S. antiterrorism campaign in the wake of the September 11 attacks. *November 13–15.* Meets with President Bush in Washington, D.C., and at Bush's ranch in Crawford, Texas, about cooperating on international issues.

2002    *January.* The last independent national TV station is forced to shut down by government. It is later rein stated after Kremlin-backed managers join the station. *May.* A nuclear weapons reduction treaty is signed by Russia and U.S. *October.* About 120 innocent theater-goers are killed after Chechen rebels storm the theater and hold those inside hostage. *December.* Suicide bombers kill more than 50 in an attack on the government building in Grozny.

2003    *May–August.* Suicide bombers attack around the country. Chechen rebels are held widely responsible.

2004    *March.* President Putin wins election in a landslide. Moscow-backed Chechen president, killed in 2004 attack. *May.* Chechen President Akhmad Kadyrov killed in a bomb blast in Grozny. *September.* More than 300 people killed during the siege of a school in Beslan. President Putin does away with elections for regional governors and plans to appoint them himself.

2005    *January.* Protests take place around the country in response to cuts in benefits to elderly. *February.* Government opponents call for a vote of no-confidence in response to the protests.

*June.* The government takes control of gas company Gazprom.

*September.* Plans to build a gas pipeline under the Baltic Sea are sealed between Russia and Germany.

2006     *March.* Putin signs economic agreements with China, agreeing to supply the country with Russian gas.

*July.* Russian special operatives assassinate Chechan warlord Shamil Basayer.

# BIBLIOGRAPHY

Shevtsova, Lilia, *Putin's Russia*, Washington, D.C., Carnegie Endowment for International Peace, 2003.

Jack, Andrew, *Inside Putin's Russia: Can There Be Reform Without Democracy*? New York: Oxford University Press, 2004.

Baer, Peter and Glasser, Susan, *Kremlin Rising: Vladimir Putin's Russia and the End of Revolution,* New York: Scribner, 2004.

CNN.com

Nytimes.com

Businessweek.com

Freerepublic.com

# FURTHER READING

Albats, Yevgenia. *The State Within a State: The KGB and Its Hold on Russia—Past, Present, and Future.* Trans. Catherine Fitzpatrick. New York: Farrar, Straus & Giroux, 1994.

Brown, Archie, and Lilia Fedorovna, eds. *Gorbachev, Yeltsin, and Putin: Political Leadership in Russia's Transition.* Washington, DC: Carnegie Endowment for International Peace, 2001.

Matthews, John R. *The Rise and Fall of the Soviet Union* (World History Series). San Diego, Calif: Lucent Books, 2000.

McFaul, Michael. *Russia's Unfinished Revolution.* Ithaca, NY: Cornell University Press, 2001.

Pavlovic, Zoran. *Russia.* New York: Chelsea House Publishers, 2007.

Pearson, Raymond. *The Rise and Fall of the Soviet Empire.* New York: St. Martin's Press, 1997.

Putin, Vladimir, with Nataliya Gevorkyan, Natalya Timakova, and Andrei Kolesnikov. *First Person: An Astonishingly Frank Self-Portrait by Russia's President.* Trans. Catherine Fitzpatrick. New York: Public Affairs, 2000.

Rose, Richard, and Neil Mundro. *Elections Without Order: Russia's Challenge to Vladimir Putin.* New York: Cambridge University Press, 2002.

Shiraev, Eric, and Vladislav Zubok. *Anti-Americanism in Russia: From Stalin to Putin.* New York: Palgrave, 2000.

# PHOTO CREDITS

page:

| | | | |
|---|---|---|---|
| Frontis : | Associated Press, AP | 69: | Associated Press, AP |
| 14: | Associated Press, AP | 73: | Associated Press, AP |
| 18: | Associated Press, BRITISH WAR OFFICE | 79: | Associated Press, POOL |
| 24: | Associated Press, AP | 83: | Associated Press, AP |
| 29: | Corbis | 87: | Associated Press, EPA POOL |
| 33: | Corbis | 93: | Presidential Press Office, Russia |
| 34: | Corbis | 97: | Associated Press, AP |
| 40: | Associated Press, AP | 99: | Associated Press, ITAR TASS |
| 43: | AFP/Getty Images | | |
| 53: | Getty Images | 102: | Associated Press, PRESIDENTIAL PRESS SERVICE |
| 55: | Associated Press, AP | | |
| 58: | Associated Press, AP | 105: | Associated Press, AP |
| 62: | Library of Congress, Prints and Photographs Division | 108: | Associated Press, AP POOL |
| 65: | Associated Press, AP | | |

Cover: © President of Russia/The Presidential Press and Information Office

# INDEX

# About the Authors

**CHARLES J. SHIELDS** is the author of 35 books for young people, primarily histories and biographies. His 1988 book, *The College Guide for Parents* (The College Board), won a Distinguished Achievement Award from the Educational Press Association. In 1995, he was recognized by the state of Illinois as one of "Those Who Excel in Education." Until 1997, he was chairman of the English department at Homewood-Flossmoor High School in Flossmoor, Illinois. Since then, he has been writing full-time.

**BRENDA LANGE** has been a journalist, author and public relations professional for 20 years. She graduated summa cum laude from Temple University in Philadelphia and is a member of the American Society of Journalists and Authors. This is the sixth book she has written or revised for Chelsea House.

**ARTHUR M. SCHLESINGER, JR.** is the leading American historian of our time. He won the Pulitzer Prize for his books *The Age of Jackson* (1945) and *A Thousand Days* (1965), which also won the National Book Award. Professor Schlesinger is the Albert Schweitzer Professor of the Humanities at the City University of New York and has been involved in several other Chelsea House projects, including the series *Revolutionary War Leaders*, *Colonial Leaders*, and *Your Government*.